A Practical Guide To Your Human Rights and Civil Liberties

Dr Michael Arnheim
Barrister at Law
Sometime Fellow of St John's College, Cambridge

Straightforward Publishing
www.straightforwardco.uk

Copyright © Dr Michael Arnheim 2017

Dr Michael Arnheim has asserted the moral right to be identified as the author of this work.

All rights reserved. No part of this publication may be reproduced in a retrieval system or transmitted by any means, electronic or mechanical, photocopying or otherwise, without the prior permission of the copyright holders.

978-1-84716-673-9

Printed by 4edge www.4edge.co.uk

Cover Photograph: Copyright House of Lords 2016 / Photography by Roger Harris

Whilst every effort has been made to ensure that the information contained within this book is correct at the time of going to press, the author and publisher can take no responsibility for any errors or omissions contained within.

Contents

Preface

1. Where do your Human Rights come from?   7

2. A Fistful of Fallacies   42

3. Your Right to Life   60

4. The Prohibition of Torture   87

5. Your Right to Freedom of Expression   109

6. Do you have a Right of Privacy?   143

7. From Rights to Privileges   166

8. Your Right to a Fair Trial   198

9. Rights vs. Rights   221

10. Q&A – A Socratic Dialogue   253

Index

PREFACE

This book is appearing at a critical time for Britain – and for your human rights as a law-abiding member of society. The winning slogan of the "Leave" campaign to take Britain out of the EU was "Take Back Control" – supposedly including taking back control of human rights law from the European Court of Human Rights in Strasbourg, which was blamed for expanding the scope of the European Convention on Human Rights (ECHR) in a "politically correct" direction. However, it turns out that Brexit is not going to free the UK from the toils of Strasbourg or the ECHR after all. Not that that makes any difference, because the UK domestic courts are not obliged to follow Strasbourg decisions slavishly in any event but only to take them "into account". The fact that UK domestic judges-- with some notable exceptions -- tend to follow the Strasbourg line is their own choice. This is not going to change after Brexit – unless the Government takes corrective action by passing legislation through Parliament to curb judicial activism, which is not at all likely.

Your human rights will therefore continue to be eroded– unless you happen to belong to one of the categories favoured by "political correctness" (PC). On the other hand, if you belong to the non-PC "forgotten people" who gave out a great roar by voting "Leave" in the UK's Brexit referendum on 23 June 2016 or for Donald Trump as US President, or if you are a supporter of the growing populist movement sweeping mainland Europe, then you may one day -- not without great difficulty -- manage to roll back the PC tide that has already engulfed the "chattering classes" of the West, and in so doing you may be able to reclaim the genuine human rights to which you are entitled.

I owe a debt of gratitude to more people than I can mention, and not least to my friends Jack Ward, Rosie Craig, Shola Awoderu and Brian Abramson, and also to my publisher, Roger Sproston, who has performed yeoman service in preparing the book for publication.

This is my nineteenth published book to date. Two previous titles were also on human rights:

The Handbook of Human Rights Law, Kogan Page, London, 2004; and
The Problem with Human Rights Law, Civitas, London, 2015.

Some of my *Huffington Post* blogs also deal with human rights:
www.huffingtonpost.co.uk/author/dr-michael-arnheim

You will find my Wikipedia biography here:
https://en.wikipedia.org/wiki/Michael_Arnheim

Dr Michael Arnheim
London
15 February 2017

Chapter 1
Where Do Your Human Rights Come From?

Where do your human rights come from? Which begs the question: Where do rights in general come from? Which begs the yet further question: What exactly *is* a right?

Philosophers and other theorists have long had a field day debating the meaning of "rights", but this exercise tends to produce more heat than light. In this book I am more concerned to view rights from a practical point of view. But it will do no harm to start at least by quoting a current accepted academic definition of "rights" from the *Stanford Encyclopedia of Philosophy*: "Rights structure the forms of our governments, the contents of our laws, and the shape of morality as we perceive it." So far, so good.

But this somewhat pompous pronouncement offers no explanation of where rights come from, though it does at least provide us with a threefold classification of rights – rights connected with government, legal rights and moral rights. Here are a few examples:

- The right to vote in elections – a political right associated with government.
- The right to remain silent – a legal right that is particularly relevant to criminal law.
- The right to expect courteous treatment by others – a moral right.

We are now ready to explore the provenance of rights, in order to test their validity.

Natural Rights

There has been a long tradition of belief in natural or God-given rights (which are not necessarily synonymous), or imprescriptible or inalienable rights, meaning absolute rights that do not depend on any grant and are irremovable. Such concepts can be traced back to Ancient Greece, and there has been no shortage of theories in support of them in modern times. But it is important to stress that these theories without more have no practical effect and do not entitle anyone to claim any rights – regardless of what the academic proponents of such theories may say. Nevertheless, I will spend a little time just putting these ideas into context.

The concept of natural rights is closely associated with belief in natural law, which was famously defined by the Roman statesman and philosopher Cicero: "True law is right reason in agreement with nature, universal, unchangeable and eternal, which calls us to duty by its commands and restrains us from wrongdoing by its prohibitions." But how can we tell whether a particular dictate is indeed in accordance with nature? There is no answer to this conundrum. Slavery, for example, was taken for granted by Cicero as natural, though he believed that slaves should be treated humanely, and he is known to have freed some of his own slaves, notably Tiro, who served as his secretary both as a slave and later after he was emancipated. After Cicero's death Tiro was able to buy an estate near Puteoli, probably from a bequest left to him by his former master, and it was Tiro who was instrumental in publishing his former master's collected works before he himself died at the age of 99. But the fact remains that Cicero regarded slavery as part of the natural order – which no modern believer in natural law would accept. But slavery is only one issue on which upholders of natural law disagree with one another. Other such issues include abortion, the rights of the unborn child, contraception, homosexuality and the whole question of equality. This goes to show just how vague and imprecise the content of natural law is, which makes it impossible to base anything on it.

St Thomas Aquinas, the famous medieval Catholic philosopher and theologian who combined Christianity with ancient Greek philosophical thought, notably that of the great Greek philosopher Aristotle, largely identified natural law with divine law, seeing divine law as essentially natural law with the infusion of scriptural revelation. "Natural law," he declared, "prescribes virtuous actions, since everyone's reason naturally dictates to him to act virtuously." Aquinas identified the four cardinal natural virtues as prudence, temperance, justice and fortitude, to which he added the three theological virtues of faith, hope and charity.

There is no shortage of modern natural law/natural rights protagonists, one of the best known of whom is Professor John Finnis of Oxford with his theory of "practical reasonableness" in his book titled *Natural Law and Natural*

Rights, in which he states: "Almost everything in this book is about human rights ("human rights" being a contemporary idiom for "natural rights": I use the terms synonymously)" [page 196]. This is totally unhelpful to anybody wanting to understand human rights from a practical legal point of view.

The most famous statement of natural rights is contained in the American Declaration of Independence of 1776, which proclaims the right of the thirteen colonies to claim *"the separate and equal station to which the Laws of Nature and of Nature's God entitle them"* – a neat identification of natural law with divine law. From there it is but a short step to natural rights, in the ringing attestation: *"We hold these truths to be self-evident, that all men are created equal, that they are endowed by their Creator with certain unalienable Rights, that among these are Life, Liberty and the pursuit of Happiness."* The rights identified here are said to be God-given and at the same time self-evident, i.e. obvious and therefore natural. But, in spite of the Declaration's august status in the American pantheon (and the efforts of self-styled "declarationists"), it does not actually confer any rights as such and cannot be invoked in a lawsuit.

"Nonsense upon stilts"

Perhaps the last word on natural rights should go to Jeremy Bentham (1748-1832), the famous utilitarian philosopher and positivist jurist. Natural rights, according to Bentham, are "simple nonsense: natural and imprescriptible rights, rhetorical nonsense,—nonsense upon stilts." So-called moral and natural rights are mischievous fictions and anarchical fallacies that encourage civil unrest, disobedience and resistance to laws, and revolution against established governments. Only political rights, those positive rights established and enforced by government, have "any determinate and intelligible meaning." Rights are "the fruits of the law, and of the law alone. There are no rights without law—no rights contrary to the law—no rights anterior to the law." [Jeremy Bentham, *Anarchical Fallacies*, 1796].

In short, according to Bentham the only real rights are those conferred by positive law, which in the British context meant essentially legislation passed by Parliament.

Common Law

The Common Law is often defined as "judge-made law". This is completely wrong. The making of laws is *legislation*, which is reserved to Parliament. The judges' function is only to interpret and apply the law. But judges do not always respect their proper boundaries, indulging instead in "judicial activism" or even "judicial supremacism". The problem really began with the well-known case of the snail in the bottle, *Donoghue v. Stevenson* [1932] UKHL 100. But it has become a much more serious problem in the past thirty years or so, and shows no sign of abating.

In the "snail" case Mrs Donoghue was treated to a ginger beer by an unnamed friend at Minchella's café in Paisley, Scotland. Minchella poured some of the ginger beer into a tumbler, and Mrs Donoghue had consumed most of it when a semi-decomposed snail floated into view. As a result, Mrs Donoghue claimed that she suffered from shock and severe gastroenteritis. Then as now, ginger beer came in an opaque bottle, so it was not possible to spot the snail in advance.

Because the ginger beer was ordered and paid for not by herself but by her friend, Mrs Donoghue had no contract with Minchella and therefore could not sue him. Her friend could have sued Minchella but had suffered no loss. So Mrs Donoghue's ingenious Scottish lawyer took a flyer and sued the manufacturer, Stevenson in the tort of negligence. Mrs Donoghue lost her case in Scotland and it eventually went on appeal to the House of Lords, where it was heard by five judges. Here Mrs Donoghue unexpectedly won, thanks to an alliance between Lord Atkin, a maverick Australian Welshman, and two Scottish law lords, but the two English law lords, Lord Buckmaster and Lord Tomlin, dissented strenuously.

Mrs Donoghue won her case on the basis of what Lord Atkin called the "neighbour principle", which he had just made up! He summarized his extremely broad made-up "principle" in these words: "You must take reasonable care to avoid acts or omissions which you can reasonably foresee would be likely to injure your neighbour. Who, then, in law is my neighbour? The answer seems to be – persons who are so closely and directly affected by my act that I ought reasonably to have them in contemplation as being so affected when I am directing my mind to the acts or omissions which are called in question." This over-broad "principle" wreaked havoc with the law of negligence, from which it has still not recovered.

In his dissenting opinion, Lord Tomlin correctly held that there was "no material from which it is legitimate for your Lordships House to deduce such a principle" as Lord Atkin's made-up "neighbour principle". The settled law at the time was quite simple: a manufacturer was liable to a user of his product with whom he did not have a contract only if the product was dangerous in itself or if it became dangerous as a result of a latent defect. Ginger beer did not fall into either of these categories. In his dissenting opinion, Lord Buckmaster laid down the true position of the law in a sharp reprimand to Lord Atkin: *"The law applicable is the common law, and, though its principles are capable of application to meet new conditions not contemplated when the law was laid down, these principles cannot be changed nor can additions be made to them because any particular meritorious case seems outside their ambit."* This is still a correct statement of the law today, but it has been lost sight of with the rise of judicial activism or indeed judicial supremacism.

What Lord Buckmaster was saying was not that the principles of the common law could never be changed but that they could not be changed by judges in order to accommodate a case with which they happened to be sympathetic – which is exactly what happened in the *Donoghue* case.

Twenty years after the "snail" case Lord Denning was rightly taken to task by Viscount Simonds, who excoriated

Denning's "purposive interpretation" of an Act of Parliament as "a naked usurpation of the legislative function under the thin disguise of interpretation". [*Magor & St Mellons Rural DC v. Newport Corp* [1952] AC 189]. Even today there are still a few leading judges who are prepared to stand up against this kind of judicial usurpation. See for example the recent UK Supreme Court case of Prince Charles's Letters. [*R (Evans) v. Attorney General* [2015] UKSC 21], which was concerned with freedom of information. In a strong dissenting opinion, Lord Wilson pointed out that in reaching its decision the majority "did not in my view interpret section 53 of the Freedom of Information Act. It rewrote it. It invoked precious constitutional principles, but among the most precious is that of parliamentary sovereignty, emblematic of our democracy".

So, if not by judges, how can the principles of the common law be changed? Answer: by Parliament. The most fundamental principle of the UK Constitution is the Sovereignty of Parliament. This is not in dispute. In its "Brexit" decision of 3 November 2016 the three-judge panel of the Divisional Court of Queen's Bench (with Lord Chief Justice Thomas of Cwmgiedd presiding) unanimously held that: "The most fundamental rule of the UK's constitution is that Parliament is sovereign and can make and unmake any law it chooses." This was later amended to read: "It is common ground that the most fundamental rule of UK constitutional law is that the Crown in Parliament is sovereign and that legislation enacted by the Crown with the consent of both Houses of Parliament is supreme (we will use the familiar shorthand and refer simply to Parliament). Parliament can, by enactment of primary legislation, change the law of the land in any way it chooses. There is no superior form of law than primary legislation, save only where Parliament has itself made provision to allow that to happen." [*R (Miller) v. Secretary of State for Exiting the European Union* [2016] EWHC 2768 (Admin)]. On 24 January 2017, the majority on the UK Supreme Court put the position slightly differently: "The law is made in or under statutes, but there are areas where the law has long been laid down and developed by judges themselves, that is the common law. However, it is not open to judges to apply or develop the common law in a way which is inconsistent with the law as laid down in or under statutes, i.e. by Acts of Parliament. This is because Parliamentary sovereignty is a fundamental principle of the UK constitution...." [*R (Miller) v. Secretary of State for Exiting the European Union* [2017] UKSC 5].

The Divisional Court's formulation is preferable to that of the Supreme Court, which exaggerates the historical role of the judges, though even this formulation carefully eschewed claiming that the judges "made" law, contenting itself with the phrase that the common law had long been "laid down and developed" by judges. The Divisional Court formulation is also to be preferred for unequivocally describing the Sovereignty of Parliament as *the* most fundamental rule of the UK constitution, as against the Supreme Court's description of Parliamentary sovereignty as merely "*a* fundamental principle of the UK constitution" (my emphasis).

The United States also has a common law system. But in most states of the United States the common law has been codified by the state legislature, leaving little room for state judges to usurp the legislative function. Sir William Blackstone, an English judge and Oxford professor, pioneered a codification of the common law in his four-volume *Commentaries on the Laws of England* (1770), modeled on the Roman Emperor Justinian's *Institutes*. Blackstone's compilation formed the basis of the American codifications of the common law, but the UK Parliament has never shown any inclination to follow suit – a gross dereliction of duty. The counterpart in the social sciences to the scientific postulate "Nature abhors a vacuum" may well be expressed as: a *dereliction* of duty by one party invites *encroachment* by another. Parliament's total failure to codify the common law or even regularize it in anything other than in a piecemeal way left the door open for the judges to step in.

So What?

What, you may ask, is wrong with that? The answer is, everything. For one thing, when judges make law it is inevitably vague and uncertain, as against legislation by Parliament, which is detailed and precise and prepared by professional parliamentary draftsmen. For the disastrous consequences of Lord Atkin's attempt at lawmaking in *Donoghue v. Stevenson*, see M. Arnheim, "Five Centuries of Legal Thinking", *The Eagle*, St John's College, Cambridge, 2011. The recent resort by some justices of the UK Supreme

Court to what they call "common law fairness" is another good example of vague lawmaking. In *Osborn v. Parole Board* [2013] UKSC 61, involving claims by three convicted prisoners for an oral hearing, Lord Reed defined "the circumstances in which fairness requires an oral hearing" in these terms: "Generally, the board should hold an oral hearing whenever fairness to the prisoner requires such a hearing in the light of the facts of the case and...the importance of what is at stake." [§81]. In other words, fairness requires an oral hearing whenever fairness to the prisoner requires an oral hearing! – which, besides being tautologous, makes the mistake of looking at the situation from the prisoner's point of view alone, instead of balancing against the prisoner's interests those of the public, in whose interests the prisoner was incarcerated in the first place.

The second argument against judge-made law is that, unlike laws passed by Parliament, judge-made law lacks any democratic underpinning. But the most worrying aspect of judge-made law is that it tends to be "politically correct", which favours certain special interest groups at the expense of the law-abiding majority of the population.

Common Law Rights

Among the time-honoured common law rights are the following, most of which have been whittled down as a result of judicial decisions:
- *Every right has a reciprocal obligation:* An important principle, which has unfortunately largely been lost

sight of. As an ordinary law-abiding member of society you have numerous obligations, including the obligation to pay heavy taxes – and, if you are male, even the duty to lay down your life for your country if called up in wartime. In return for all this the government owes you the paramount duty of protection and national security, delivery of which is all too often hampered by "politically correct" court decisions..

- *Nobody ought to be a judge in his own cause* [From the Latin: *Nemo debet esse judex in causa sua*]: This fundamental principle of natural justice designed to prevent judicial bias has not been as fully implemented in Britain as it should have been and as it has been in most other jurisdictions. For one thing, amazingly enough, an application for a judge to recuse himself or herself (i.e. to stand down from a particular case) is initially made to that very same judge! Lord Justice Sedley has wittily pointed up the paradox of "a judge who, in order to decide whether he will be sitting as a judge in his own cause, has to sit as a judge in his cause". [Sedley, "When should a judge not be a judge? Recuse yourself." LRB vol 33 No. 1 (6 January 2011)].

- *Hear the other side [*From the Latin: *Audi alteram partem]:* This is the other most fundamental principle of natural justice, meaning that both parties to a legal dispute have the right to be heard in the interests of justice. However, this is another right which is honoured more in the breach than in the observance, partly because of the difficulty poor litigants have to obtain legal aid, and also because of the system of the loser paying the winner's (largely uncontrolled) costs, so that a claim for £10,000 can end up costing the losing party £100,000 – a deterrent to prospective claimants from going to court.

- *The presumption of innocence:* This right is now enshrined in ECHR Article 6, but it has a long pedigree, going all the way back to Roman law, from which it was absorbed into the Common Law. But once again, ordinary people are not always able to avail themselves of this right. Innocent people who are arrested on suspicion of murder or sex crimes without any basis are quite likely to find themselves presumed guilty and the subject of massive media interest while their false accusers are protected by anonymity. Also, a "Not Guilty" verdict in a criminal court is not the same as innocent, because it is quite possible for a guilty person to be acquitted on a technicality.

- *Habeas corpus* (literally, "You may have the body"): A very ancient common law "writ" -- actually a privilege rather than a right -- which came to be enshrined in an act of Parliament, the Habeas Corpus Act 1679, most of which was subsequently repealed, leaving it to the judges to interpret as they pleased. As a result, this area of the law, which is bedevilled by issues related to terrorism, is in a state of disarray.

- *Privacy*: There is no right of privacy under the Common Law. In the well-known case of *Gorden Kaye v Robertson* [1990] EWCA Civ 21, the Court of Appeal correctly eschewed the temptation to create a common law right of privacy and called upon Parliament to pass appropriate legislation – a call which, needless to say, was not heeded. Instead, later judges reinterpreted the unrelated law of c*onfidence or confidentiality* so as to cover privacy – with a less than satisfactory result. ECHR Article 8 has also come to be stretched to cover privacy in certain circumstances, although all it actually protects is everyone's "right to respect for his private and family life", which is not at all the same thing as privacy.

- *Prenuptial Contract*: Contract law is in general one of the more stable and settled areas of the common law, but even here there are some exceptions. Prenuptial agreements are a case in point. These are contracts entered into prior to and in contemplation of marriage. They have long been recognized in a number of European countries and in the United States, where every state has a statute (yes, actual legislation!) regulating such contracts. But in Britain it has been left to the judges, who until 2010 set their faces resolutely against recognition of prenuptial contracts. One such agreement has now been recognized by the courts –

which, significantly, was in the interests of a wealthy wife. Whether a prenuptial agreement protecting a wealthy husband would ever be recognized by an English court remains to be seen. It would represent a watershed in a divorce-law regime which lopsidedly favours wives over husbands.

- *National Security*: It is important to realize that national security does not just protect the rights of the Government but the human rights of every single law-abiding member of the population as well. This fundamental truth is nowadays all too often lost sight of by the courts. But that has not always been the case. See for example, the *Hosenball* case. [1977] 3 All ER 452, in which Lord Denning, who was not averse to making up the law when it suited him, showed that he took national security seriously. So, has the law changed since then? Actually not, but it has been reinterpreted to the point of reinvention in a "politically correct" direction.

Magna Carta

There has long been a lot of hype surrounding Magna Carta ("the Great Charter"), the first version of which dates from 1215. There are few documents in history which have been the subject of more hype than Magna Carta, which is often depicted as a stepping stone to "democracy". In fact, however, it was nothing of the kind, but rather a failed attempt to settle a dispute between the king and the barons, although it was reissued in 1216 after King John's death, pruned of its most extreme provisions. Further slightly amended versions were ratified in 1217, 1225 and 1297.

Magna Carta was the product of a conflict between King John (reigned 1199-1216) and the barons, whom the king had cut out of top positions at court and on the *Curia Regis*, the King's Council, preferring to rely on "new men". King John was also concerned about justice for ordinary people and used to sit in judgment himself even in some comparatively minor cases. His reforms were welcomed by many free tenants, who were now able to rely on the legal system against the barons. Needless to say, the barons were less keen on John's reforms for this very reason!

What Magna Carta Really Says

To get a more balanced view it will help to look at the actual wording of the most relevant clauses.
[www.bsswebsite.me.uk/History/MagnaCarta]:

- **1215 version, clause 2:** "We have also granted to all the free-men of our kingdom, for us and our heirs forever, all the liberties written out below, to have and to keep for them and their heirs, of us and our heirs."
  Comment: (a) The adulators of Magna Carta tend to gloss over the important little word, "free-men" (or "freemen"). The term included merchants, lawyers and free landowners, plus some peasants. Peasants made up the majority of the population, but the majority of

the peasantry were not freemen. "Freemen" are estimated to have accounted for only about one seventh of the population [Arlidge, Anthony & Igor Judge, Magna Carta Uncovered, 2014: 47]. (b) It is also worth mentioning that this is one of only five clauses of the original Magna Carta to have survived to the present day. The rights now apply to everyone, but they do not mean much (see below).

- **1215 version, clause 39**: "No free-man shall be seized or imprisoned, or dispossessed, or outlawed, or in any way destroyed; nor will we condemn him, nor will we commit him to prison, excepting by the legal judgment of his peers, or by the laws of the land." Comment: (a) This is the most celebrated clause of Magna Carta and is another of the five clauses to have survived to the present day. Once again, the undertaking applied at the time only to "freemen".

- **Trial by Jury:** Clause 39 is also often seen as a guarantee of trial by jury. This is not the case. In fact, juries existed even in Anglo-Saxon times, but these were investigative juries, prototypes of the grand juries still found in the United States but no longer in England. (b) *"The legal judgment of his peers"* meant that people were to be judged by others of the same rank. It was in accordance with this that until 1948 members of the peerage of the United Kingdom had the right to trial by the House of Lords rather than by a "common jury" selected from the general population or even a so-called "special jury" of wealthier property owners (abolished generally in 1949 and for commercial trials in the City of London in 1971).(c) Although this clause now supposedly applies to everyone, in England there are plenty of crimes for which a sentence of imprisonment can be imposed by magistrates, without the option of trial by jury. And juries in civil cases have all but disappeared – while in the US trial by jury is still alive and well in civil as well as criminal cases, and guaranteed by the US Constitution.

- **1215 version, clause 40:** *"To none will we sell, to none will we deny, to none will we delay right or justice."* This is yet another of the five surviving clauses. But delay is still endemic in the present-day English legal system, and the costs system is such as to deny justice to many litigants in civil cases.

- **1215 version, clause 60**: "Also all these customs and liberties aforesaid, which we have granted to be held in our kingdom, for so much of it as belongs to us, all our subjects, as well clergy as laity, shall observe towards their tenants as far as concerns them." This clause, which is repeated in the 1216, 1217, 1225 and 1297 versions, is the king's attempt to impose the same obligations on the barons towards their vassals as the king owed to the barons, showing the king's concern for the lower orders over against the barons.

- So, with exception of clause 39, as discussed above, people below the rank of baron got short shrift from Magna Carta, all the versions of which, including the final definitive version of 1297 ratified by Edward I (r. 1272-1307), are chiefly concerned with the relationship between the Crown and the barons, which continued to fester.

The Equality Act 2010

This mammoth piece of legislation, running to 218 sections plus no fewer than 28 schedules, just goes to show that Parliament *can* produce composite and wide-ranging legislation when it wants to. The only problem is that this particular law is a piece of doctrinaire "political correctness" which does little to benefit the law-abiding majority of the population. Even its title is a misnomer. Instead of "Equality Act" it should more accurately be labelled "Privileges Act", because it confers special privileges on certain favoured elements. It was passed in the dying days of Gordon Brown's Labour Government, receiving the Royal Assent on 8 April 2010, less than a month before that government's humiliating defeat and its replacement by a Conservative-Liberal Democrat coalition, which however allowed this monstrosity to stand.

The Act is chiefly intended to tackle "discrimination", both "direct" and "indirect", against certain "protected characteristics", namely: (a) age, (b) disability, (c) gender reassignment, (d) race (e) religion or belief, (f) sex and (g) sexual orientation. But not all these "protected characteristics" are given equal protection: there is a hierarchy of protection. For example, treating someone differently on account of their age is not discrimination if you can show that your treatment of them is "a proportionate means of achieving a legitimate aim" [section 13(2)]. Privilege is clearly revealed in the Act's treatment of disability According to section 13(3) of the Equality Act: *"If the protected characteristic is disability, and B is not a disabled person, A does not discriminate against B only because A treats or would treat disabled persons more favourably than A treats B."* In other words, treating disabled people more favourably than non-disabled people does not count as discrimination against the non-disabled people. So much for "equality".

Compare this with the sensible approach adopted by the House of Lords as a court in *London Borough of Lewisham v. Malcolm* [2008] UKHL 43, – decided under the Disability Discrimination Act 1995. Mr. Malcolm, who was suffering from schizophrenia, was a council tenant. In breach of his lease, he sublet and moved out of his council flat. This destroyed his security of tenure and gave the council an unanswerable claim to possession. To defeat that claim Mr Malcolm's legal representatives relied on section 22(3)(c) of the Disability Discrimination Act 1995, which provided that: "It is unlawful for a person managing any premises to discriminate against a disabled person occupying those premises...by evicting the disabled person, or subjecting him to any other detriment." This argument failed at first instance, succeeded in the Court of Appeal, but was rejected again by a unanimous House of Lords. Lord Brown put his finger on the fact that the law was moving from non-discrimination to privilege: "What is the obligation placed upon landlords towards the disabled under the Disability Discrimination Act 1995? Is the obligation to treat the disabled no less favourably than those not disabled? Or is it to treat them more favourably? That is the central question for your Lordships' determination on this appeal. Nowadays – since the 2005 amendments to the Act – in certain respects a landlord must treat the disabled more favourably." The House of Lords restored the trial judge's conclusion "that there was no causal link between Mr. Malcolm's schizophrenia and his subletting of the flat". The Equality Act 2010 has now moved the law into more "politically correct" territory, so it is quite likely that the sensible decision in Malcolm would not be repeated.

"Support Gay Marriage"

Though "religion or belief " is supposedly a "protected characteristic" under the Equality Act 2010, it is easily trumped by "sexual orientation", as in the case of the Belfast Christian bakery owners who were found to have discriminated against a gay would-be customer by refusing to bake a cake proclaiming "Support Gay Marriage". [*Lee v. McArthur* [2016] NICA 29 -- decided by the Northern Ireland Court of Appeal on the basis of Northern Ireland law, which was essentially the same as English law]. This decision subordinated to gay rights not only the Christian bakery owners' rights in regard to religion but also their right to freedom of expression and their right as a business to accept or reject a particular order. At the time of writing, the case was about to be heard by the UK Supreme Court, which had already found against Christian businesspeople in a more justifiable case involving sexual orientation. In that case the Christian proprietors of a hotel were held to have discriminated against a gay couple in a civil partnership by refusing the couple accommodation in a double room in their hotel. (*Bull v. Hall* [2013] UKSC 73).

Political Correctness - Stages

The Equality Act is in fact only the latest of a long list of "politically correct" anti-discrimination laws, which are all swept up in the Equality Act itself. "Political correctness" tends to go through the following stages:

- *Anti-discrimination legislation*, e.g. the Sex Discrimination Act 1975.
- *Positive or reverse discrimination*: When that does not work in practice, e.g. because fewer women tend to seek election to Parliament, reverse discrimination (or "affirmative action") is introduced, as in the Sex Discrimination (Election Candidates) Act 2002, which exempted the selection of parliamentary candidates from the provisions of the Sex Discrimination Act 1975 and allowed political parties to select candidates based

on gender. This Act contained a "sunset clause" making it expire at the end of 2015, but it was extended by section 105(3) to the end of 2030.

- *Quotas*: When even that does not work in practice, the next step is to resort to the use of *quotas*. In the case of female representation in Parliament, this was done by means of all-women shortlists. In fact, the Labour Party used all-women shortlists even before the 2002 Act. In the 1997 general election, all-women shortlists were used in half of all winnable seats, although the practice had already been held to be illegal under the Sex Discrimination Act 1975 by an industrial tribunal in January 1996. The Conservative Party and Liberal Democrats used more indirect methods of increasing the number of female Members of Parliament. The Speaker's conference of the House of Commons in July 2009 called for at least half the new candidates at the next general election to be women, together with increased numbers of ethnic minorities and people with disabilities. The 2015 general election produced the highest number of women MPs ever, 191 or 29% of the total of 650. This amounted to 21% of all Conservative MPs and 43% of all Labour MPs. Ann Widdecombe MP put her finger on the problem with all-women shortlists with her comment in 2008 that they created "special privileges" for women, not "equal opportunities". And it should be added that all-women shortlists discriminate against men.

It has to be stressed that female politicians (or would-be politicians) are just one of several groups to be accorded special privileges as a result of the "politically correct" mindset that has gained control amongst the ruling elite, both political and legal, in recent years.

The Human Rights Act 1998

The Human Rights Act (HRA) 1998 (which came into force in the year 2000), introduced by Tony Blair's Labour Government, incorporated most of the articles of the European Convention on Human Rights (ECHR), making them part of UK law. Prior to that, although the UK had been a signatory to the Convention since 1951, access to the Convention could only be had by applying to the European Court of Human Rights in Strasbourg after all UK domestic remedies had been exhausted. The Human Rights Act has made it possible to claim under the ECHR directly to any UK court, but it still remains possible to take your case to Strasbourg after all domestic remedies have been exhausted.

Section 6(1) of the HRA provides that: "it is unlawful for a public authority to act in a way which is incompatible with a Convention right." The term "public authority" includes "a court or tribunal". This may appear to enable the public to keep control of the courts. That is not correct. If anything, this provision gives an extra fillip to the already tremendous power exercised by the judiciary. What it really means is that judges can effectively scupper any law that they consider to be "incompatible" with the ECHR. Judges are not allowed to declare a law void or invalid on the ground that it is incompatible with a Convention right. All they can do is issue a "declaration of incompatibility", leaving it up to the Government to decide whether they want to ask Parliament to repeal or amend the offending legislation. But in practice such a declaration consigns the legislation in question to outer darkness.

Anyone can bring a claim against a "public authority" for *violating* their rights under any article of the ECHR. As usual, there is no proper definition of "public authority". Section 6(3) of the HRA looks at first sight as though it is going to define "public authority": "In this section 'public authority' includes – (a) a court or tribunal, and (b) any person certain of whose functions are functions of a public nature, but does not include either House of Parliament or a person exercising functions in connection with proceedings in Parliament." Section 6(5) then says: "In relation to a particular act, a person is not a public authority by virtue only of sub-section (3)(b) if the nature of the act is private." None of this adds up to a definition of "public authority", as the word used is "includes" rather than "means". And what is meant by "certain of whose functions"? Which ones? This is far too vague to be of any real help. It leaves a void at the heart of the Act, which can only be filled by the judges. And judicial definitions are rarely precise.

In other words, what should be an elementary preliminary question turns out to be yet another of the many issues up for grabs in the courts. Is, for example, a statutory sewerage undertaker a "public authority"? Yes. What about the RSPCA? No. [See M. Arnheim, *Handbook of Human Rights Law*, p. 6].

And, needless to say, the test for a "public authority" under the HRA is not the same as that for a "public body" exercising "public decision-making powers" under the general law applicable to judicial review. Most, but not all, human rights cases are decided by judicial review, which does not assist you as a claimant.

Shortly after the HRA came on stream in 2000 a few senior judges took it upon themselves to define the HRA as a "constitutional" statute with "entrenched" status, meaning that the ECHR rights incorporated into the HRA were to be "accorded a higher normative status than other rights" – like a Bill of Rights in countries with a written constitution like the USA. The conclusion drawn from all this was that, as a "constitutional" statute equivalent to a "Bill of Rights", adjudication under the HRA "needs to be approached generously in order to afford citizens the full measure of the protection of a Bill of Rights. By contrast, decisions taken day by day by commercial judges in respect of the meaning of, say, standard forms of letters of credit may sometimes employ relatively strict methods of construction." [Lord Steyn, paper kindly sent to the author by Lord Steyn based on a lecture given by him on 19 October 2000]. I criticized this whole argument in my *Handbook of Human Rights Law* first published in 2004, p. 64ff. First, judges have no right to rank Acts of Parliament in some sort of hierarchy. The fundamental principle of the Sovereignty of Parliament means that no legislation is "entrenched" and *any* Act of Parliament, however important, can be amended or even repealed by another Act of Parliament. As the premise that the HRA is "entrenched" is incorrect, so it is illogical to conclude that interpretation of the ECHR rights must be less strict than in ordinary commercial cases. Who would benefit from such a "generous" and less strict interpretation of the ECHR rights anyway? It is a mistake to think that this would benefit ordinary law-abiding members of the public. On the contrary, it is precisely this kind of "mission creep", which has been occurring in recent years that benefits special interest groups, including terror suspects, asylum seekers and even convicted killers.

The European Convention on Human Rights (ECHR)

It is important to note that the ECHR does not give or confer any rights. It treats the rights as already existing. That is why the preamble to the HRA refers to them as "rights and freedoms guaranteed under the ECHR." The preamble to the ECHR itself talks about "the maintenance and further realization of human rights and fundamental freedoms". The term "further realization" is worrying, though, because this leaves open the possibility of extending the rights further – which has in fact happened, though only in the interests of special interest groups (see above).

There has been widespread recognition of the dangers of this "mission creep", but blame for it has generally been misplaced: attributed to the Strasbourg court rather than to the domestic UK courts, who are really largely responsible. In a speech delivered on 25 April 2016, two months before the EU referendum, Theresa May declared: "If we want to reform human rights laws in this country, it isn't the EU we should leave but the ECHR and the jurisdiction of its Court", which she wrongly described as "in effect a final appeals court" but which she rightly blamed for delaying the extradition of Abu Hamza and for "almost" stopping the deportation of Abu Qatada. She contrasted the ECHR and its Strasbourg court with Britain:

"This is Great Britain – the country of Magna Carta, Parliamentary democracy and the fairest courts in the world – and we can protect human rights ourselves in a way that doesn't jeopardise national security or bind the hands of Parliament. A true British Bill of Rights – decided by Parliament and amended by Parliament – would protect not only the rights set out in the Convention but could include traditional British rights not protected by the ECHR such as the right to trial by jury."

Needless to say, that speech predated Theresa May's miraculous conversion to "Brexit" on the way to 10 Downing Street, which was followed by an announcement that there were no plans to withdraw from the ECHR!

Theresa May's distorted view of human rights law was largely the same as that expressed in the Conservative Party's strategy paper titled "Protecting Human Rights in the UK" published in October 2014. This attacked the "mission creep" affecting the ECHR, which was blamed squarely on the Strasbourg court: "There is mounting concern at Strasbourg's attempts to overrule decisions of our democratically elected parliament and overturn the UK courts' careful applications of convention rights."

That the ECHR has been badly affected by politically correct "mission creep" is undeniable. And it is also true that the Strasbourg court was in the vanguard of this "politically correct" development. But the domestic UK courts were not far behind. It is important to realize that the UK courts are not bound to follow Strasbourg, only to "take into account" Strasbourg judgments and decisions. [HRA section 2(1)(a)]. Lord Irvine, a former Lord Chancellor, has pointedly remarked that the UK domestic courts have proceeded "on the false premise that they are bound (or as good as bound) to follow any clear decision of the ECtHR which is relevant to a case before them....The judges are not bound to follow the Strasbourg court: they must decide the case for themselves." [Lord Irvine, "A British Interpretation of Convention Rights", lecture, 14 December 2011]. On the whole, with a few notable exceptions, the UK domestic judges have behaved as if bound by Strasbourg – and have sometimes even out-Strasbourged Strasbourg. [See M. Arnheim, *The Problem with Human Rights Law*, Civitas, 2015].

"Unconscious Bias"

In a remarkable recent admission, Lord Neuberger, president of the UK Supreme Court, remarked, referring to judges: "I dare say that we all suffer from a degree of unconscious bias, and it can occur in all sorts of manifestations. It is almost by definition an unknown unknown, and therefore extraordinarily difficult to get rid of, or even to allow for. But we must, as I have said, do our best in that connection as in every other." This is undoubtedly true, but the "unconscious bias" that Lord Neuberger appears to be thinking of is against those who are poor, foreign or uneducated. ["Fairness in the courts: the best we can do", address to the Criminal Justice Alliance, 10 April 2015]. But the real problem is quite different: it is an "unconscious bias" deriving from a politically correct mindset, which tends to favour those elements in society that are perceived as underprivileged, together, strangely enough, with terrorist suspects and even convicted killers.

Referring to public law cases in general, that acute observer of the relationship between the judiciary and the executive, Professor J.A.G. Griffith, observed: "The idea that judges can be politically neutral in such cases has never been true." ["The Brave World of Sir John Laws," *Modern Law Review* 63 (2000) 159]. A radical socialist and a democrat who strongly opposed judicial supremacism as anti-democratic, John Griffith mercilessly attacked the judiciary in his book *The Politics of the Judiciary* (1977), which ran to five editions. At that time the judiciary was largely essentially conservative and reluctant to attack the government. But towards the end of his long life (he died in 2010 at the age of 91) Griffith, realizing that the legal climate had changed and that judicial activism was on the rise, tackled it head-on in several hard-hitting long articles. Here is a quotation from one of these: "[T]he proposals advanced by Sir John Laws openly advocate a massive shift of power from the executive and Parliament to the judiciary. The political question is whether or not this is to be supported, whether it is likely to result in a society more just, more free, more equal." ["The Brave World of Sir John Laws," *Modern Law Review* 63 (2000) 159 at 173.]

Griffith was in little doubt that the answer to this question was in the negative, and the evidence of the past sixteen years of judicial decision-making supports his view, although it has to be said that since that time Sir John Laws himself has to his credit actually become something of an exemplar of judicial restraint. He took issue, for example, with Lord Bingham's remark in *R (Ullah) v. Special Adjudicator* [2004] UKHL 26 that, "The duty of national courts is to keep pace with Strasbourg jurisprudence as it evolves over time." Sir John Laws fired back: "So the House of Lords and the Supreme Court have accorded overriding force to the notion that only Strasbourg's rulings on the Convention are 'definitive' or 'authoritative'. Why should this be so?....I have, in common with others, come to think that this approach [treating Strasbourg decisions as authoritative] represents an important wrong turning in our law." [Lord Justice Laws,

Lecture III, The Common Law and Europe, Hamlyn Lectures 2013, 27 November 2013].

However, the leaven of "political correctness" informed by the "unconscious bias" discussed above is still very much in the ascendant not only in the judiciary but also in the "chattering classes" as a whole, which will undoubtedly ensure the continued dominance of "political correctness" in the judiciary for the foreseeable future.

Separation of Powers

As we have seen, there is continued recognition of the Sovereignty of Parliament as the bedrock of the British Constitution, which is salutary, but how does that relate to the doctrine of the separation of powers, which is also generally accepted as an important constitutional principle. It was famously defined by Lord Diplock in the following terms: "It cannot be too strongly emphasized that the British constitution, though largely unwritten, is firmly based upon the separation of powers: Parliament makes the laws, the judiciary interpret them." [*Duport Steels v. Sirs* [1980] 1 All ER 529]. This clearly recognizes that the judiciary should not be involved in law-making. A fuller explanation of the separation of powers was provided by Lord Mustill in 1995: "It is a feature of the peculiarly UK conception of the separation of powers that Parliament, the executive and the courts each have their distinctive and largely exclusive domain. Parliament has a legally unchallengeable right to make whatever laws it thinks right. The executive carries on the administration of the country in accordance with the powers conferred on it by law. The courts interpret the laws and see that they are obeyed." [*R (Fire Brigades Union) v. Secretary of State for the Home Department* [1995] 2 AC 513]. By contrast, there is no shortage of incorrect constitutional formulations, including the much-quoted version by Lord Justice Nolan in the case of *M v. Home Office* [1992] QB 270: "The proper constitutional relationship of the executive with the courts is that the courts will respect all acts of the executive within its lawful province, and that the executive will respect all decisions of the courts as to what its lawful province is." This is alarmingly wrong, because it suggests that the courts have the power to determine the extent of the power of the executive. This is *legislation*, and therefore a matter for Parliament, not for the courts. [It is worth recalling that it was also in this case that another Court of Appeal judge, Lord Donaldson MR, came out with the unintentionally comical observation that the Crown had no legal personality – an elementary error, which is obviously disproved by the fact that every criminal prosecution is brought in the name of the Crown].

The basis of the separation of powers is that it establishes a system of checks and balances, which however was lost as a result of the Constitutional Reform Act 2005, which represents the complete capitulation of the executive, in the person of the Lord Chancellor, who actually has to take an oath to uphold and protect the independence of the judiciary without any reciprocal oath or undertaking of any kind on the part of the judiciary to respect the executive.

Another important aspect of the system of checks and balances inherent in the separation of powers that has been lost is the appointment of the judiciary by the executive – a very important democratic feature which is still an important feature in the US Constitution. In the UK the appointment of judges was transferred by that much unpublicized Constitutional Reform Act 2005 to what can only be termed a Quango – well away from public scrutiny, unlike the US system, in which appointment of the top judges is entrusted to the President (the head of the executive) subject to confirmation by the Senate (a branch of the legislature).

An aspect of the checks and balances inherent in the separation of powers which remains unchallenged but very sparingly used is the power of Parliament to override or abrogate any court decision, even with retroactive force if it so decides. This is what happened in the case of *Burmah Oil v. Lord Advocate,* which ruled that the UK Government had to pay compensation for ordering the Burmah Oil Company to destroy oil fields in Burma to prevent them from falling into the hands of the Japanese. Parliament immediately abrogated this ruling by passing the War Damage Act 1965, which obtained the Royal Consent on 2 June 1965. It was amusing to see a reference to the Burmah Oil case in the UK Supreme Court's "Brexit" decision in January 2017. Needless to say, there was no mention of the fact that the House of Lords court decision was overridden by Parliament. There are some recent court decisions crying out for similar treatment, for example the UK Supreme Court decision in *Belhaj v. Straw* [2017] UKSC 3. However, the do-nothing government of Theresa May lacks the courage to take any such action, which has not even been mooted.

*****

CHAPTER 2
A Fistful of Fallacies

British human rights law is surprisingly vague and uncertain. As a result, there is room for divergent approaches to the law. What is particularly worrying is a "liberal" approach best described as "politically correct" which favours certain special interest groups -- including those perceived as underprivileged together with terror suspects, asylum seekers and even convicted killers -- at *your* expense as a member of the law-abiding majority of the population. What is even more disquieting is that this "politically correct" approach to the law is now in the ascendant, enjoying support not only among the judges of the European Court of Human Rights in Strasbourg but also, with some notable exceptions, among UK domestic judges.

In the USA people are very conscious of the different approaches to the law adopted by different Supreme Court justices. A presidential election is almost as much about future appointments to the Supreme Court as about the next occupant of the White House. It comes as no surprise to Americans that "liberal" justices tend to indulge in "judicial activism" or even "judicial supremacism", while conservative justices are more likely to practice judicial self-restraint. [See Michael Arnheim, *US Constitution for Dummies*].

A similar dichotomy is actually in existence in Britain, but it is hardly noticed, as the dominant "liberal" or "politically correct" tendency is usually attributed to the judges of the Strasbourg court or the European Court of Justice in Luxembourg rather than to their emulators among the UK domestic judges. But it is actually not difficult to understand why a "liberal" or "politically correct" take on the law should be associated with a more assertive attitude generally, tending towards "judicial activism" or even "judicial supremacism".

"Liberal" or "politically correct" judges almost by definition give themselves more latitude to interpret the law as they see fit, which can easily spill over into their encroaching on the preserve of the executive and even the legislature, especially in the face of a Government and Parliament whose dereliction of duty over hundreds of years has failed to recognize that it is their own duty to regularize the common law by means of legislation. As a result of this dereliction of duty on the part of the government and Parliament, a vacuum has opened up into which unelected judges who are responsible to nobody are almost inevitably drawn, resulting in "judicial activism".

Why middle-aged middle-class judges should now be adherents of "political correctness" is not as puzzling as it may at first sight appear, as was shown in Chapter 1. The combination of a supine Government and Parliament coupled with "political correctness" among the judiciary leads almost inevitably to "judicial activism", which in turn leads inexorably to "judicial supremacism".

So What?

But why should that worry you? Those nice judges protect your rights against the big bad government, don't they? Yes, especially if you are a terror suspect, an asylum seeker or a convicted killer. And, in a case not involving any of those categories, you can expect to be favoured if you belong to any of the groups protected by the Equality Act 2010: especially females, minorities, gays, "trans" people and the disabled.

Human Rights Hype

There's a good deal of hype -- or indeed propaganda -- surrounding human rights. The human rights lobby or civil rights industry is anxious to persuade you that your human rights are protected by their "politically correct" approach to the law, which is not the case at all.

Rights vs. Rights

This "generous" approach to human rights fails to recognize that *all* human rights cases involve human rights on *both* sides: human rights vs. human rights – yes, even when it is a case against the government about, say, national security. National security is not just some abstract concept: it represents the interests and, yes, the human rights, of every law-abiding member of the population. The emphasis by the courts tends to be on the rights of the claimant. For example, a case involving a terror suspect objecting to deportation as a violation of his rights under ECHR Article 3 (prohibition of torture or inhuman or degrading treatment or punishment) tends to be viewed by the courts almost exclusively from the terror suspect's point of view without realizing that there are human rights on the other side as well – the human rights of every single law-abiding member of society. Weakening national security is often hailed as a human rights victory, but that is exactly the opposite of the truth. It may well represent a victory for the human rights of certain special interest groups, but it will be a defeat for the human rights of the majority and may in the long-run undermine the whole democratic underpinnings of UK society.

The Kerensky Syndrome

An important case in point is the so-called "Belmarsh 9" case, in which a full bench of nine law lords decided by an 8-1 majority that the indefinite detention of foreign prisoners without trial under the Anti-Terrorism, Crime and Security Act, section 23 was not in keeping with human rights law. [*A(FC) v. Secretary of State for the Home Department* [2004] UKHL 56].

Lord Hoffmann held that the section was incompatible with the British constitution as a whole. He also expressed the view that the necessary condition for the legislation -- that there was a public emergency threatening the life of the nation -- was non-existent:

96. This is a nation which has been tested in adversity, which has survived physical destruction and catastrophic loss of life. I do not underestimate the ability of fanatical groups of terrorists to kill and destroy, but they do not threaten the life of the nation. Whether we would survive Hitler hung in the balance, but there is no doubt that we shall survive Al-Qaeda....Terrorist violence, serious as it is, does not threaten our institutions of government or our existence as a civil community. 97. In my opinion, such a power in any form is not compatible with our constitution. The real threat to the life of the nation, in the sense of a people living in accordance with its traditional laws and political values, comes not from terrorism but from laws such as these. That is the true measure of what terrorism may achieve. It is for Parliament to decide whether to give the terrorists such a victory.

Lord Hoffmann's complacent dismissal of the seriousness of the terrorist threat is disquieting, especially when compared with warnings sounded by the security services themselves. In a rare speech, Alex Younger, the head of MI6 described the threat posed by Islamic State or Daesh (Al-Qaeda's successor terrorist organization} as "unprecedented", adding without any qualification: "There will be terrorist attacks in this country." Since 2014 the UK threat level has been set at "severe", just one down from the highest level, "critical". [Ewen MacAskill – *The Guardian*, 22 December 2016].

The familiar liberal argument is that over-reacting to the threat of terrorism with harsh provisions will do greater damage to British democracy than anything that the terrorists could do. Yet, how democratic is it for judges to determine whether there is "a threat to the life of the nation", a political question? By arrogating this power to themselves the judges were arguably encroaching on the preserve of the executive government or even of Parliament.

Lord Walker, the one law lord who supported the Government's position, sensibly argued that the provisions for indefinite detention were "necessary" and accompanied by "several important safeguards against oppression". He therefore held that the relevant legislation was "proportionate, rational and non-discriminatory". And the very fact that there could be such major differences between judges on the same panel (including differences among the majority as well) only goes to show just how flimsy a legal basis the majority decision rested on. But even Lord Walker made the mistake of identifying "human rights" only with the rights of the claimants: "All these safeguards seem to me to show a genuine determination that the [relevant legislation] should not be used to encroach on human rights any more than is strictly necessary." What about the human rights of the majority of law-abiding members of society, which would be protected by the legislation?

One of the chief objections of the majority in the House of Lords was to the differential treatment of British and foreign prisoners, the provisions for indefinite detention being applied solely to foreign prisoners. The case originated with a decision by the Special Immigration Appeal Commission (SIAC) to deport the nine foreign prisoners on the basis that there was evidence that they posed a threat to national security. So, why were they not simply deported? This was itself the result of a wrong interpretation of ECHR Article 3 by the Strasbourg court in *Chahal v. UK* [1996] ECHR 54, which ruled that the UK could not deport a foreigner if he "would face a real risk of being subjected to treatment contrary to Article 3 (torture or inhuman or degrading treatment or punishment) if removed to another State." (See also the same interpretation of Article 3 in regard to extradition in *Soering v. UK* (1989) 11 EHRR 439). There is in fact absolutely no reason other than judicial activism for interpreting Article 3 in that way. Why, after all, should the UK be responsible for a foreign country's treatment of someone who was being deported from the UK? This is clear not only from Article 3 itself but also from the specific wording of ECHR Article 1, which obliges the states, including the UK, to "secure to everyone *within their jurisdiction* the rights and freedoms defined in" the articles including ECHR Article 3 (emphasis added). This makes it clear that the UK's obligations in regard to Article 3 apply only within the UK itself.

This "liberal" approach endangers democracy in two ways: first, by allowing unelected judges to arrogate powers to themselves to which they are not entitled; and secondly and even more importantly, by sapping the resources of the state to tackle terrorism. This is what I have termed the "Kerensky syndrome". Alexander Kerensky was the democratic Prime Minister of Russia after the February Revolution 1917. As a liberal and a democrat he was not prepared to crack down on Lenin's revolutionary Bolsheviks, who therefore took advantage of Kerensky's weakness to stage a coup, known as the October Revolution 1917. Kerensky managed to escape with his life and spent the next 50 years in exile scratching his head in puzzlement over the death of Russian democracy.

Zero-Sum Game

Recognition that even a national security case involves human rights on both sides should lead to the further recognition that human rights law is a zero-sum game, meaning that the rights of the winning side detract from the rights of the loser. So, for example, if, as frequently happens, a terror suspect is prevented by the courts from being deported, his right to remain at large in the UK (even if constrained to some extent by having to wear a tag of some kind) diminishes the rights of all law-abiding members of society, who are endangered to some extent by this decision. Similarly, a railwayman's right to strike will impact the rights of the public to use public transport, and a junior doctor's right to strike could even affect his patients' right to life.

"The Rule of Law"

"The rule of law" is one of the most popular slogans put about by the "politically correct" lobby. The term has a long history, but its recent provenance is from the phrase popularized by John Adams, one of the American founding fathers and second

President of the United States: "A government of laws and not of men". So important was this doctrine to John Adams that he introduced it into the Massachusetts Constitution of 1780.

But laws are just words on paper. So how can they govern? They are inevitably subject to interpretation – by courts, judges and lawyers. An anonymous wag early on put his finger on this truth and retorted: "A government not of men but of laws? No, a government not of laws but of lawyers." Despite the obvious truth of this trenchant riposte, Adams's doctrine is still regularly trotted out, not only in America but also in Britain and elsewhere, in its shorthand form, "the rule of law", as a touchstone of democracy. But the wag's throwaway line has proved prophetic.

A Fistful of Fallacies

There are a good many fallacies concerning human rights put about by what may be called the "civil liberties lobby". A good source is the website of the organization known as "Liberty", which includes a section titled "Human Rights Act mythbuster". The "myths" assembled there are actually mostly true. It is the arguments marshalled *against* these "myths" that are myths – or fallacies. Let's look at some of these supposed "myths":

- **"The Human Rights Act undermines parliamentary sovereignty."** Needless to say, the Liberty website pooh-poohs this serious assertion and goes even further: "Our Human Rights Act actually increased

British sovereignty" – because the Human Rights Act (HRA) enables human rights cases to be decided by the UK courts without resorting to Strasbourg. "Today, British judges rule on all claims arising in the UK – and help to influence Strasbourg case law." The truth is almost exactly the opposite. The Strasbourg court has grown increasingly "politically correct" (PC), making up the law as it goes along – and UK judges have largely followed suit, even though *making law, or legislation*, is for Parliament, not for the courts: the courts are only supposed to *interpret* the law.

- **"Under the Human Rights Act, British courts are bound by the European Court of Human Rights in Strasbourg."** The Liberty website dismisses this out of hand. It points out (correctly) that "British courts are not required to **follow** the judgments of the European Court of Human Rights blindly – they must only **'take account'** of them." But it then adds, less correctly: "Domestic judges can – and often do – depart from Strasbourg case law, to take account of the UK's own laws and traditions." The true position, as stated by Derry Irvine, a former Labour Lord Chancellor, is that the UK domestic courts have proceeded "on the false premise that they are bound (or as good as bound) to follow any clear decision of the ECtHR which is relevant to a case before them." [Lord Irvine, "A British Interpretation of Convention Rights", lecture 14 December 2011]. Do UK judges ever

51

depart from Strasbourg rulings? Yes, but more often to out-Strasbourg Strasbourg than the opposite. An alarming example of this is the House of Lords decision in *AF v. Secretary of State for the Home Department* [2009] UKHL 28, in which the appellant terror suspects claimed that they had been denied a fair trial under ECHR Article 6 because of the judge's reliance on secret material. Lord Irvine (who was already retired by this time) commented: "The House unanimously allowed the appeal, and in so doing clearly proceeded on the premise that it was obliged to do so." Lord Hoffmann, who is himself not uncritical of the Strasbourg court, said: "I think that the decision of the ECtHR was wrong, and that it may well destroy the system of control orders which is a significant part of this country's defences against terrorism. Nevertheless, I think that your Lordships have no choice but to submit." Lord Hoffmann's reason for this *non sequitur* was that "the United Kingdom is bound by the convention, as a matter of international law, to accept the decisions of the ECTHR on its interpretation." Lord Rodger of Earlsferry made the same point even more briefly: "Even though we are dealing with rights under a UK statute, in reality we have no choice. Argentoratum locutum, iudicium finitum – Strasbourg has spoken, the case is closed." Besides disagreeing with the sentiment expressed here, I would amend the Latin to read: *Argentorato locuto, iudicium finitum.* Lord Irvine's comment is direct and authoritative: "I beg to differ. Section 2 of the HRA means that the domestic court *always* has a choice. Further, not only is the domestic Court entitled to make the choice, its statutory duty under s.2 obliges it to confront the question whether or not the relevant decision of the ECHR is sound in principle and should be given effect domestically. Simply put, the domestic Court *must* decide the case for itself." (Emphasis added). [See Arnheim, *The Problem with Human Rights Law*, Civitas, 2015].

- **"Interpretation of the European Convention as a 'living instrument' undermines the intentions of the postwar founders."** The Liberty website, not surprisingly, stresses the need for interpretation of the convention to evolve "as modern life and social attitudes change", adding: "In the UK judicial interpretation is an essential part of our Common Law tradition – and no Bill of Rights around the world can exist without it." This glosses over the crucial difference between *interpretation* and *legislation*: it is the courts' job to interpret the law but not to change it. Legislation is the preserve of the legislature, Parliament. The dividing line between the two is a bit blurred at the edges, but not nearly so much as the advocates of judicial activism like to claim.

- **"The Human Rights Act does nothing for ordinary people."** The true position is that, though couched in the language of universal human rights, the ECHR and HRA as interpreted by the courts subordinate the rights of ordinary people to those of special interest groups, including supposedly disadvantaged people, asylum seekers, illegal immigrants, terror suspects and even convicted killers. Needless to say, the Liberty website is anxious to claim that "our Human Rights Act protects everyone's human rights". The right which is highlighted is "privacy", a right that is not actually mentioned in the ECHR or the HRA, which only protects everyone's "right to respect for his private and family life, his home and his correspondence". And, unless you are a "celebrity" who can get a "super-injunction", you are likely to be at the mercy of the media moguls, who are specially protected by the UK HRA, which goes a lot further than the ECHR. [See Chapters 6 and 7].

- **"People now have a 'human right' to anything."** I have never heard anyone make this claim, which Liberty pillories as a "myth", probably on the ground that this claim paints the HRA as too "liberal". The truth is that everyone has the right to do anything that is not specifically prohibited. So, for example, you have the right to pick your nose in public – an ugly and unhygienic habit but one which is perfectly legal. Because English law is in such disarray, a challenge to the exercise of some unprohibited right can easily turn into an ugly court battle. The right of public nudity is an example.

- **"The Human Rights Act protects only criminals and terrorists – it does nothing for victims."** Liberty dismisses this out of hand – and adds that "most freedoms can be limited in the interest[s] of public safety, to protect national security, or to prevent an offence being committed." The trouble is that the courts -- including the UK domestic courts -- tend to interpret the ECHR in such a way as to endanger public safety and national security rather than to protect it. [See second bullet point above for an example]. Terrorist suspects and even convicted killers are the darlings of the court. Just ask the parents of the murdered little James Bulger! [See Chapter 3].

- **"Human rights have been imposed on us by Europe."** Liberty is right to reject this assertion, but fails to address the real problem. The ECHR, as Liberty point out, which was adopted by the Council of Europe in 1950, was largely drafted by English lawyers. The UK signed up to it in 1951, and in 1998 it was incorporated into UK law through the HRA. The problem though is that the ECHR has been misinterpreted and misapplied by "politically correct" Strasbourg judges, whose rulings have largely been followed by UK judges.

- **"The Human Rights Act has made us all less safe. It needs amending so that the courts are required to balance our rights to safety and security."** Liberty won't have any of this, stressing that the HRA already requires the courts to balance human rights against the interests of public safety. Unfortunately, Liberty fails to recognize that the true "balancing act" is not between human rights and public safety but between human rights and human rights: the favour shown by the courts to terror suspects and convicted killers is not just at the expense of some abstract concept called "national security" but at the expense of the human rights of each and every law-abiding and peace-loving UK resident. And it is also important to realize that human rights are a zero-sum game: the more rights that are enjoyed by terror suspects and convicted killers, the less there are left for the law-abiding and peace-loving majority.
- **"The Human Rights Act has cost the British taxpayer millions – and been a goldmine for lawyers."** Liberty reject this too, pointing out that, with the Human Rights Act it is no longer necessary for human rights cases to be decided by Strasbourg. They can now be heard by British courts, "which is far more efficient and cost-effective". Anybody who has had any experience of the British courts will be either amused or surprised by this description of their operation. In fact, the costs awarded by the Strasbourg court are

generally quite modest, while the costs awarded by the UK courts are often enormous, completely uncontrolled – and generally paid for by the British taxpayer no matter which side wins. And the fact that these cases can be decided by the domestic courts does not prevent repeated repeals in addition to trips to Strasbourg. The case of Abu Qatada is a recent case in point. [See Arnheim, *The Problem with Human Rights Law*].

- **"British Common Law and Magna Carta protected our rights long before the Human Rights Act."** Liberty is here caught on the horns of a dilemma. On the one hand they do not want to knock the long tradition of British human rights, but they insist at the same time that the HRA improved everything. The truth is that the significance of Magna Carta, dating from 1215, has been blown up out of all proportion and that one of its few surviving clauses is still a dead letter. This is the promise by the government in clause 40 that "to none will we deny, to none will we delay right or justice". [See Chapter 1, above, and Arnheim, *Two Models of Government*, p. 201]. As for the human rights previously protected under the Common Law, they have shrunk rather than been enhanced by the HRA, as Liberty would have us believe. Freedom of speech is a good example of this. Two hundred years ago Britain was a bastion of free speech, as can be seen, for example, from the audacious cartoons of

Gillray and Rowlandson, which mercilessly mocked even the King and the royal family. Today, thanks to the special privileges accorded to the press by the HRA (not the ECHR) and the rise of political correctness, which exerts a muzzling effect even on ordinary speech – most recently on the use of gender-specific pronouns like "he" and "she". [See Chapter 6].

- **"The Human Rights Act gives too much power to unelected judges."** Liberty makes the point that the HRA does not give the courts the power to strike down laws but only to issue a "declaration of incompatibility". This is true, but the effect is in practice hardly different. Liberty, predictably, goes on to sing the praises of the judiciary: "One of the cornerstones of our democracy is our independent judiciary, interpreting and applying the law. Judicial decision-making is fundamental to the rule of law, and the powers given by our Human Rights Act to the courts fall squarely within this historic framework." The truth is that the UK's unelected -- and, as far as the higher courts are concerned, practically irremovable-- judges have arrogated to themselves much more than their proper function of interpreting and applying the law. Increasingly in recent years they have been encroaching on the preserve of Parliament by *making* law, which amounts to *judicial supremacism*. "Europe", however defined, is a convenient readymade scapegoat for this tendency. But the truth is that the rise of judicial activism and its development into judicial supremacism is largely the product of home-grown "political correctness", which is not limited to human rights cases. A particularly striking example of it is provided by the Supreme Court case about Prince Charles's letters to Tony Blair as Prime Minister, which was based entirely on UK law. Two members of the Court had the courage to express a trenchant dissent.

****

CHAPTER 3
Your Right To Life

Principles

ECHR Art 2(1) declares: *Everyone's right to life shall be protected by law.* This makes it clear that the right to life is *not* conferred or guaranteed by this article. The right exists already, but it is the duty of the state to protect that right by law. Art 2(2) enumerates as exceptions to this right: lawful executions (no longer permitted), self-defence, arresting a fleeing suspect and quelling riots and insurrections.

The Charter of Fundamental Rights of the European Union is structured rather differently from the ECHR. The UK has a "derogation" from the Charter, whose effect (if any) is open to debate. But the Charter will in any event presumably cease to apply to the UK if or when a full "Brexit" occurs. The Charter is made up of 54 articles grouped under seven Chapters. The "Right to life" is Article 2 in Chapter I, "Dignity". Article 2 reads: "*1. Everyone has the right to life. 2. No one shall be condemned to the death penalty, or executed.*" This chapter also contains two other articles that are not paralleled in the ECHR: "Article 1, Human Dignity", and "Article 3, Right to the integrity of the person." The relevant provision in the Universal Declaration of Human Rights is very brief: Article 3: "Everyone has the right to life, liberty and security of person."

Case Studies

How is the basic principle of your right to life to be applied? If your life is at imminent risk from the criminal activities of someone else, a public authority that is aware of the risk should take action to protect you – and if you're killed, the public authority that failed to protect you should be held responsible. That at least is the way it's meant to work. In practice it's not quite so simple.

Osman v. UK (1998)

The Strasbourg court case of *Osman v. United Kingdom* [(1998) 29 EHRR 245] is a good example. After a long series of bizarre incidents to which the police were called, a schoolteacher shot and killed Ali Osman and seriously wounded his son. "Why didn't you stop me before I did it?" pleaded the distraught teacher on his arrest. "I gave you all the warning signs." Were the police liable for the shootings? The English courts held that the police enjoyed immunity from suit in cases alleging negligence for failure to investigate or suppress crime. However, the Strasbourg court found unanimously that this purported immunity amounted to a violation of the right to access to justice contained in ECHR Article 6(1), but the claim under Art 2 still failed.

Clunis v. Camden & Islington Health Authority (1998) QB 978

This is another sad and bizarre case. Jonathan Zito was innocently standing with his brother on the platform at

Finsbury Park tube station when he was attacked and fatally stabbed in the eye by Christopher Clunis, a paranoid schizophrenic who had been in and out of mental hospitals for the previous six years. This lawsuit was brought not by the victim's family but, surprisingly, by Clunis, who was seeking damages from the health authority for professional negligence in allowing him to be at large! His argument in simple terms was that had he been confined to a psychiatric hospital he would not have killed Jonathan Zito.

His claim was rejected on several grounds, notably the ancient principle stated by Lord Mansfield in the case of *Holman v. Johnson* (1775): "A court will not lend its aid to a man who founds his cause of action on an illegal or immoral act."

Keenan v. UK [2001] ECHR 242

Mark Keenan, a convicted prisoner with psychiatric problems, hung himself a day after he had assaulted two prison guards. His mother took the case all the way to Strasbourg, claiming failure to protect Mark's right to life under ECHR Article 2. The Court dismissed the claim, finding that because his record contained no formal diagnosis of schizophrenia, the authorities could not have known that he was an immediate suicide risk. Mark's mother was nevertheless awarded £10,000 in damages plus legal expenses of £21,000 under ECHR Article 3 (inhuman and degrading treatment) and ECHR Article 13 (lack of effective remedy).

Savage v. South Essex Partnership **[2008] UKHL 74**
Anna Savage's mother, a mental patient detained under section 3 of the Mental Health Act 1983, absconded from an NHS hospital and committed suicide. The first instance High Court judge held that the test to establish a breach of ECHR Article 2 was gross negligence. The Court of Appeal rejected this, and the House of Lords, the highest court, unanimously held that as there was a "real and immediate" risk of suicide, the hospital was in breach of Article 2. This accorded with the coroner's jury's finding that "the precautions in place....to prevent Mrs Savage from absconding were inadequate."
Rabone v. Pennine Care NHS Trust [2012] UKSC 2
Taking this a step further, in *Rabone v. Pennine Care NHS Foundation Trust* the UK Supreme Court held that the Trust had failed in its duty to protect a woman from the "real and immediate" risk of suicide even though she was a voluntary mental patient.

Self-Defence

Unlike most of the other Convention rights, Article 2 has horizontal as well as vertical effect. In other words, it is not only concerned to protect the individual against the state but also seeks to protect individuals against one another. Article 2(2)(a) provides that *"killing in defence of any person from unlawful violence" is justifiable provided "it results from the use of force which is no more than absolutely necessary."* Does this include self-defence? This has never been tested in Strasbourg, though it has been the subject of some high-profile English domestic cases. In the best-known of these cases, Tony Martin, a farmer, shot at two intruders to his remote farmhouse, aptly named "Bleak House", killing one (aged 16) and wounding the other (aged 29): *R v. Anthony Edward Martin* [2001] EWCA Crim 2245. The prosecution claimed that Tony Martin, who had been burgled a number of times before, was lying in wait for the burglars and opened fire on them at close range without warning. Tony Martin based his case on self-defence but was convicted of murder and attempted murder and wounding with intent to cause injury, and he was sentenced to life imprisonment. On appeal his conviction was downgraded from murder to manslaughter on the grounds of diminished responsibility and his sentence was reduced from life to five years' imprisonment. In the Court of Appeal Lord Chief Justice Woolf remarked that, "Because he was being burgled at the time there was considerable public sympathy for Mr Martin and media interest in his case. There were also suggestions that the law was in need of change."

This was an understatement. There was an outcry over Tony Martin's conviction and he became something of a popular hero, which led eventually to a change in the law of self-defence. When Tony Martin was convicted of murder the test was "reasonable force" – the householder could not use more than reasonable force against an intruder. This was eventually amended by section 43 of the Crime and Courts Act 2013. The law now is that a householder may use "disproportionate force" against an intruder provided the householder believes that the amount of force that he has used is "reasonable" in the circumstances, but the use of "grossly disproportionate" force by a householder is no defence.

This amendment to the law is couched in convoluted gobbledygook language, and leaves it up to the courts to decide whether the force involved was "disproportionate" or "grossly disproportionate" – arguably a distinction without a difference. But even this inconsequential change in the law applies only to self-defence in your own residence. It does not extend to defending yourself from attack on the street, preventing crime or protecting property. It is hard to say what effect, if any, the change in the law will have.

In September 2012, before the law was amended, Andy and Tracey Ferrie of Welby in Leicestershire were burgled in their home by four intruders in the middle of the night. Andy Ferrie fired at the burglars with a legally-owned shotgun and was arrested for causing grievous bodily harm to two of the alleged intruders. In the wake of the Tony Martin case, the Crown Prosecution Service had the good sense to drop the case against Mr Ferrie – but not before he and his wife had been subjected to 66 hours of police detention. After a month-long "living nightmare" the Ferries moved out of their house and emigrated to Australia. [*The Telegraph*, 26 September 2012].

Would they have fared any better under the 2013 law? It is hard to say.

"Death on the Rock"

What protection does the law give to UK security services in their fight against terrorism? Answer: Hardly any. And their work, risking their lives for Crown and country, exposes them to charges of murder and other serious crimes themselves.

In 1995 the UK was taken to the European Court of Human Rights (ECtHR) in Strasbourg for an alleged breach of ECHR Article 2 arising out of the death in Gibraltar of three members of an "active service unit" of the Provisional Irish Republican Army (IRA) at the hands of the crack British anti-terrorism unit known as Special Air Service (SAS), which had been tipped off about an impending terrorist attack in Gibraltar: [*McCann v. UK* (1996) 21 EHRR 97]. Two of the three IRA members had convictions for offences involving explosives and the third was regarded by the SAS as an expert bomb-maker. The three IRA members, Daniel McCann, Mairead Farrell and Sean Savage, were sighted by the SAS staring from a distance at a white Renault car in a carpark in Gibraltar. The SAS regarded the car as a "suspect car bomb", and "considered that it was likely that the suspects would detonate the bomb if challenged, that they would be armed and would be likely to use their arms if confronted". The Gibraltar police commissioner accordingly decided that the three suspects should be arrested on suspicion of conspiracy to murder. However, this did not happen. Instead, the three suspects were shot dead by the SAS. The European Commission of Human Rights, a preliminary body to the

Strasbourg court itself, found that "Ms Farrell and Mr McCann were shot by Soldiers A and B at close range after the two suspects had made what appeared to the soldiers to be threatening movements...Mr Savage was shot at close range until he hit the ground and probably in the instant as or after he hit the ground...Soldiers A to D opened fire with the purpose of preventing the threat of detonation of a car bomb in the centre of Gibraltar by suspects who were known by them to be terrorists with a history of previous involvement with explosives." In the event, the suspects all turned out to be unarmed and there were no explosives in their car in Gibraltar, but Mairead Farrell had in her handbag keys to another car parked just across the Spanish border in which 64 kg of Semtex was found.

The issue before, first, the European Human Rights Commission and then the Strasbourg Court itself was whether the killing of the three IRA members violated their right to life or whether it was sanctioned under ECHR Article 2(2). In short, was the force involved "no more than absolutely necessary in defence of any person from unlawful violence? Unlike ECHR Articles 8-11, where the test is whether the infringement of the rights concerned is "necessary in a democratic society", in Article 2(2) the test is the much stricter one of showing that the infringement was "absolutely necessary".

By 11 votes to 6, rejecting the claim that the killing of the three suspects was premeditated, the Commission held that there had been no violation of Article 2, but in the Court there was a photo-finish, with 10 judges finding against the UK and 9 dissenting, the minority including the president and the four most senior members of the Court. The applicants' claims for damages were unanimously dismissed, though the UK had to pay the applicants £38,700 in costs (less 37,731 French francs).

The practical question is whether security services are permitted to pre-empt terrorist violence or whether they have to wait for a terrorist to kill them before retaliating, something normally only possible in the Hollywood Wild West!

Yet an earlier case involving suspected Irish terrorism had a different outcome. [*Kelly v. UK* (1993) 16 EHRR CD 20]. British soldiers shot at a car breaking through a roadblock, killing the driver. In a civil action brought against the Ministry of Defence it was held that, as the soldiers had reasonably believed that the car contained terrorists who had to be stopped to prevent them from committing a crime, the Ministry of Defence was not liable for the death. The dead man's father's complaint was rejected by the Strasbourg Commission, which found the soldiers' use of force "strictly proportionate, having regard to the situation confronting the soldiers, the degree of force employed in response and the risk that the use of force could result in the deprivation of life", and therefore "absolutely necessary for effecting a lawful arrest within ECHR Article 2(2)(b). The case never went to the Strasbourg Court itself.

"Bloody Sunday"

On Sunday 30 January 1972 British paratroopers shot 26 unarmed participants in an illegal march, 14 of them fatally. There have been two separate investigations set up by the British Government. The Widgery Tribunal, headed by Lord Chief Justice Widgery, reported in April 1972, in the immediate aftermath of the incident, that the soldiers had not initiated the firing, although their return fire on occasion "bordered on the reckless" and was "sometimes excessive". But Lord Widgery's conclusion was that "There would have been no deaths...if those who had organized the illegal march had not thereby created a highly dangerous situation in which a clash between demonstrators and the security forces was almost inevitable."

From the outset the Widgery report was dismissed by Irish nationalists as a "whitewash". After the initiation of the Northern Ireland peace process the British government bowed to pressure for a fresh investigation of the events of "Bloody Sunday". In 1998 a new tribunal was set up under a British law lord, Lord Saville, sitting with a Canadian judge and one from New Zealand. It took twelve years to produce its report, which was eventually published in 2010.

With the exception of senior officers, the soldiers who testified before the Widgery Tribunal in 1972 had done so anonymously. The Ministry of Defence asked for the same arrangement before the new tribunal on the ground that these soldiers' lives would otherwise be in danger. The tribunal refused this reasonable request on the ground that it "would represent a material derogation from the Tribunal's public investigative function". However, the soldiers' application for judicial review of this decision was successful. In the words of Lord Woolf MR: "When what is at stake is the safety of the former soldiers and their families...the risk is extremely significant. After all, the individual's right to life is...the most fundamental of all human rights. It does appear that the tribunal failed to attach sufficient significance to this....Examining the facts as a whole, therefore, we do not consider that any decision was possible other than to grant the anonymity of the soldiers." [*R v. Lord Saville of Newdigate* [1999] 4 All ER 860].

When the 5,000-page Saville Report came out in 2010, eleven years and £191 million later, it pinned the blame squarely on paratroopers who "lost control". The soldiers' shots, maintained the report, were not fired in response to attacks by petrol bombers or stone throwers and the protestors were not posing any threat. The report was not only accepted but even endorsed by the then Prime Minister, David Cameron, who apologized on behalf of the British Government for what had happened, describing what had been done by some British soldiers as "both unjustified and unjustifiable, it was wrong". However, the report also attracted a good deal of criticism. Stephen Pollard, a senior solicitor who had represented some of the soldiers, commented that Lord Saville's certainty in identifying individual soldiers "flies in the face of most of the evidence he heard....I am certain he cherry-picked the evidence. There is just as much evidence for the opposite conclusion." [*New Law Journal* 18 June 2010; *Telegraph* 16 June 2010].

The Ulster Unionist leader Sir Reg Empey contrasted the Saville tribunal's enquiry into the 14 deaths with the absence of any enquiries into the deaths of victims of paramilitary groups during the same period.

An example of this occurred in Belfast on "Bloody Friday", 21 July 1972, almost six months after "Bloody Sunday", bombings by the IRA during which nine people were killed, including two British soldiers and five civilians, while 130 were injured. No investigation or inquiry into "Bloody Friday" was ever conducted. But on the thirtieth anniversary of "Bloody Friday" the IRA formally apologized to the families of all the civilians that it had killed and injured. [Conflict Archive on the Internet--cain.ulst.ac.uk]. The IRA carried out no fewer than 1,300 bombings in 1972.

"Hierarchy of Victims"

One of the few Protestants to join the crowd in Derry's Guild Square when the Saville report was unveiled in 2010 told an interviewer that she still bore the scars of a no-warning IRA car bomb which killed nine people just a few months after Bloody Sunday. "As she pointed out, these deaths were largely forgotten and she was typical of many Protestants who feel Saville represented a massively costly investment in the creation of a hierarchy of victims." [*Belfast Telegraph*, 16 June 2010].

Sgt Alexander Blackman

Three Royal Marines were tried anonymously, hidden behind a screen, by a court-martial for the murder of an injured Taliban insurgent in 2011. Two were acquitted and one was convicted. This was the first time since World War II that a British serviceman had been convicted of a battlefield murder. Judge Advocate General Jeff Blackett, in charge of military courts, initially ruled that the marine's identity should not be disclosed, otherwise he would become a terrorist target. This was undoubtedly correct. But this decision was overturned by the High Court in the interests of "open justice". The marine in question, 37-year-old Sergeant Alexander Blackman, was sentenced to life imprisonment, with a minimum term of 10 years and a dishonourable discharge from the marine corps. He had joined the marines 15 years earlier and served with great courage and distinction in Northern Ireland, Oman, Iraq and Afghanistan before being deployed to Helmand Province, Afghanistan in March 2011. The Taliban insurgent whom he was accused of murdering was suspected of carrying out a series of attacks on a neighbouring command post. The insurgent was badly wounded in a helicopter strike. Blackman shot him with the words: "There you are. Shuffle off this mortal coil, you cunt. It's nothing you wouldn't do to us." Turning to his colleagues, he remarked: "Obviously this doesn't go anywhere, fellas. I've just broken the Geneva convention." He still has the support of the marine corps. Major General Ed Davis, commandant-general of the corps, said: "Our mantra of 'once a marine, always a marine' is not conditional."

Was Sergeant Blackman really guilty of murder at all? The law under which he was convicted is section 42 of the Armed Forces Act 2006, which just says that: "A person subject to service law....commits an offence under this section if he does any act that – (a) is punishable by the law of England and Wales; or (b) if done in England or Wales, would be so punishable." The Geneva Convention, which Sergeant Blackman thought he had contravened, applies only to armed conflict between two signatory nations, i.e. states.

"Vexatious Claims" Against British Troops

On 4 October 2016 it was reported that: "In a joint announcement with Sir Michael Fallon, the Defence Secretary, the Prime Minister will say that UK troops will be protected from the 'industry of vexatious claims that has pursued those who served in previous conflicts.' Mrs May and Sir Michael will say that in future conflicts Britain will opt out of the European Convention on Human Rights (ECHR), protecting our frontline forces from 'spurious' legal claims." [*The Telegraph*, 4 October 2016]. This was a reference to investigation by the Iraq Historic Allegations Team (IHAT) of almost 1,500 allegations of mistreatment and unlawful killing of Iraqis, together with a separate inquiry, Operation Northmoor, looking into more than 550 allegations of abuse in Afghanistan going back to 2005.

On 8 February 2017 Theresa May promised to reduce the number of cases being pursued by IHAT, which was estimated to have cost the taxpayer £36.3 million up to that time. Phil Shiner, a solicitor whose firm, Public Interest Lawyers (PIL), brought forward more than 2,000 allegations considered by IHAT, was struck off by the Solicitors Disciplinary Tribunal for misconduct, including five charges of dishonesty. [Paddy Dinham, www.dailymail.co.uk - 2 February 2017; Ben Farmer & Robert Mendick, www.telegraph.co.uk - 2 February 2017].

At the time of writing the Parliamentary Defence Sub-Committee was about to report. The report was expected "to question why PIL was paid by IHAT to help with its inquiries. It will also criticise the MoD for paying the firm more than £200,000 after Mr Shiner had been reported to the Solicitors Regulation Authority". [Matt Dathan--*www.dailymail.co.uk*-8th February 2017].

The only conviction to date was of a member of the IHAT team itself, a civilian investigator, a retired police officer, searching for evidence of criminal abuses by British troops in Iraq, who was charged and convicted after pretending to be a policeman by using an old warrant card to gain access to a military base. He was given a conditional discharge by a magistrates' court and ordered to pay costs of £150.
[Ben Farmer & Robert Mendick--www.telegraph.co.uk-13 December 2016].

Nearly 400 retired British service personnel are currently being investigated following a decision by the Police Service of Northern Ireland (PSNI) to re-examine 302 deaths from the

1970s and 1980s. On 14 December 2016, Defence Secretary, Michael Fallon, giving evidence before the Common Defence Committee, said: "We're not going to allow the Northern Ireland process to develop into another IHAT…" [Matt Dathan -- *www.dailymail.co.uk*–14 December 2016].

On the other hand, it was admitted on the same day by Northern Ireland Minister Kris Hopkins that the deaths of 185 British soldiers would *not* be investigated. He attacked the current system as not being "fair, balanced or equitable", adding: "The almost exclusive focus on the actions of the state is disproportionate….The status quo is not working for victims and families. I want to ensure that the balance of an investigation is rightly on the terrorists who caused so much suffering rather than on the brave soldiers and police officers who sacrificed so much to protect us." It is known that "many suspected terrorists have been granted pardons or 'comfort letters' intended to protect them against prosecution." [Ian Drury – *Daily Mail*, 14 December 2016].

The last word should go to Sir Henry Bellingham MP, a former Foreign Office minister, who secured the debate on this issue: *"All of this runs contrary to pledges made by the Prime Minister and various defence ministers. It also breaches natural justice and represents a tearing up of the military covenant. It is absolutely outrageous to try and claim some sort of parity between servants of the crown who behaved in good faith on the one hand, and terrorists and paramilitaries whose sole aim was to kill as many people as possible."* [Ibid].

Assisted Suicide

Until 1961 suicide was a criminal offence under English law. This aroused a certain amount of amusement, for what sentence can be passed on a successful suicide? As English law now stands, although suicide itself is no longer a crime, deliberately assisting someone to commit suicide is a criminal offence.

Dunbar v. Plant [1997] EWCA Civ 2167

An engaged couple made a suicide pact to kill themselves by jumping simultaneously from a ladder. In the event, the male partner died but his fiancée survived. She was not prosecuted for any criminal offence. But her fiancé's father, as administrator of his son's estate, took her to court to stop her from becoming sole owner of the house that she had shared with the dead man and from claiming on his life insurance policy, of which she was the named beneficiary. By a majority the Court of Appeal held that, though never prosecuted, she was guilty of aiding and abetting her fiancé's suicide – but decided (somewhat illogically) that in the interests of "trying to do justice between the parties" she should nevertheless be allowed to have the whole of the house and insurance moneys!

Pretty v. UK [2002] ECHR 423

Diane Pretty, a sufferer from motor neurone disease, a progressive wasting condition, wanted to die with dignity and asked her husband to assist her to end her life. As this would have constituted a criminal offence on his part under the Suicide Act 1961, Diane Pretty asked the Director of Public Prosecutions (DPP) to give an undertaking not to prosecute her husband. This request was refused. Mrs Pretty then took the unprecedented step of challenging the DPP's decision in court. The case went all the way up to the House of Lords, where her application was unanimously rejected. The right to life, it was held, did not include a right to die! Nothing daunted, Diane Pretty took her case to the ECHR in Strasbourg. Her claim was rejected there as well.

Ms B v. An NHS Hospital Trust (2002) EWHC 429 (Fam)
In sharp contrast with Diane Pretty's case was that of a tetraplegic who successfully sought to have her life-support system switched off. The contrast was all the sharper because the two cases were heard within a very short time of each other. The difference, though, was that the court was not here being asked directly to decide whether the claimant should live or die, but only whether she could herself refuse medical treatment that was keeping her alive against her will.

Two "equally fundamental" but potentially conflicting principles were identified by the High Court: that of the "sanctity of life" on the one hand and, on the other, the principle of "autonomy", the rather vague right to the integrity of one's person and property, including the right to refuse medical treatment. It has to be said, however, that neither the principle of the "sanctity of life" nor that of "autonomy" can easily be derived from either Art 2 or any other article of the ECHR.

Abortion

Abortion is not one of the exceptions to the right to life enumerated in ECHR Art 2. In Britain abortion is a right purely dependent on statute law, namely the Abortion Act 1967 (not applicable in Northern Ireland), which allows a pregnancy to be terminated if, in the opinion of two medical doctors, it has not gone beyond its 24th week and that carrying the baby to term "would involve risk, greater than if the pregnancy were terminated, of injury to the physical or mental health of the pregnant woman or any existing children of her family". For a pregnancy to be terminated any later than this is subject to the more stringent test, again in the opinion of two registered medical practitioners, "that the termination is necessary to prevent grave permanent injury to the physical or mental health of the pregnant woman", or else that the pregnant woman's life is in danger if the pregnancy is continued, or finally "that there is a substantial risk that if the child were born it would suffer from such physical or mental abnormalities as to be seriously handicapped."

The emphasis on the health of the mother is understandable enough. The one slightly unexpected feature of this legislation is the possibility of terminating a pregnancy on the grounds of a risk to the health of "existing children". Children are often jealous of a new baby, fearing that the newcomer may rob them of their parents' affection, and it is conceivable that this may affect the children's health in some way. The test, though, is that this risk must be "greater than if the pregnancy were terminated" – quite a formidable hurdle to clear.

Britain (with the exception of Northern Ireland) has largely been spared the bitter controversy over abortion that has beset the USA, though until the passing of the Abortion Act in 1967 English law contained a blanket ban on "child destruction" in the Infant Life (Preservation) Act 1929. The Abortion Act 1967 (as amended by s.37 of the Human Fertilisation and Embryology Act 1990) contains a provision that "No offence under the Infant Life (Preservation) Act 1929 shall be committed by a registered medical practitioner who terminates a pregnancy" in accordance with the Abortion Act. The 1929 Act, which is still on the statute book, made it a felony if anyone, "with intent to destroy the life of a child capable of being born alive, by any wilful act causes a child to die before it has an existence independent of its mother".

Britain has been spared the acrimonious and sometimes violent conflict over abortion that has beset the US. The main reason for this is probably the fact that whereas in Britain abortion was legalised by Act of Parliament -- the Abortion Act 1967, which began life as a private member's bill -- in America it was established by the Supreme Court as a constitutional right in the landmark case of *Roe v. Wade* (1973) without any democratic mandate. Even Justice Ruth Bader Ginsburg of the US Supreme Court, a staunch advocate of abortion rights, commented (before joining the Court) that it would have been better to wait until there was enough support to introduce abortion rights by legislation: "Heavy-handed judicial intervention was difficult to justify and appears to have provoked, not resolved, conflict."

Moreover, the reasoning of the majority on the Supreme Court in *Roe v. Wade* was less than persuasive. It was based on a supposed constitutional right of privacy. The relevant principle was encapsulated in one sentence: "The right of privacy...is broad enough to encompass a woman's decision whether or not to terminate her pregnancy." The problem is that neither a right of abortion nor a right of privacy can be inferred from the language of the US Constitution. The essential objection to it therefore is that in *Roe v. Wade* the US Supreme Court usurped the power of the legislature.

Fathers' Rights?

The one person who does not figure in the Abortion Act at all is the father. In US law the foetus is regarded as part of the mother's body, so that those in favour of abortion rights are labelled "pro-choice", meaning the woman's right to choose whether to have the baby or not. This cuts the father completely out of any decision-making in regard to abortion. The fact that the British law of abortion is statute-based would enable it to adopt a value-neutral position. However, in the absence of any statutory rights for the father, the courts have refused to accord him any recognition in the abortion process.

In *C v. S* (Court of Appeal, 25 February, 1987) a father applied unsuccessfully for a court order to prevent the unmarried mother, who was under 24 weeks pregnant at the time, from having an abortion. As required by the Abortion Act 1967, two doctors had certified that continuing the pregnancy would involve a greater risk to her health than if the pregnancy were terminated. The father, who applied both on his own behalf and on behalf of the unborn child, contended that an abortion would amount to the crime of child destruction under the Infant Life (Preservation) Act 1929. In the Scottish case of *Kelly v. Kelly* (1997) a father applied for a court order restraining his wife from having an abortion. His case was dismissed on the ground that under Scots law the foetus was part of the mother's body and had no independent right to remain in the womb. But the fact that the foetus has no rights does not need to mean that the father has none either. Why could the father not have rights of his own, simply in his capacity as a father, similar to those that a father has over minor children after birth and corresponding to a father's onerous legal obligations towards his children? In the absence of any statutory provision to this effect or any common law precedent, fathers' rights are doomed to lag well behind their obligations.

Rights of the Unborn Child

English law, in common with US law, has set its face firmly against recognizing that a foetus has any legal rights at any stage prior to birth. So, in *R. v. Tait* (1989) it was held that it was not a criminal offence under section 16 of the Offences Against the Person Act 1861 to threaten a pregnant woman with the words "I am going to kill your baby". The section makes it an offence to threaten another person "to kill that other or a third person", but it was held that the section was not applicable as the unborn child was not a "person".

In *McKay v. Essex Area Health Authority* (1982) a pregnant woman contracted rubella (German measles) and as a result gave birth to a severely disabled child, who then sued the doctor and health authority concerned for failing to advise her mother to have an abortion – what has sometimes been termed a "wrongful life" suit. It was held that although the doctor owed the mother a duty to advise her to have an abortion in these circumstances, it did not follow that he owed the unborn child a duty to terminate its life, which would have given the foetus a right to die.

At first glance *Burton v. Islington Health Authority* (1992) may appear to be at variance with this decision, but that is not in fact the case. Tina Burton, who was born disabled, sued the health authority for causing her abnormalities by carrying out a gynaecological operation on her mother while pregnant and thereby injuring Tina while still a foetus. The health authority were held negligent in not performing a pregnancy test before undertaking this procedure and had to pay Tina damages for her disability. A duty of care, it was held, is owed to a foetus although a foetus only acquires a legal personality at birth. The crucial difference between this case and *McKay* is that in *McKay* the injuries were caused by the mother's rubella, whereas in Burton they were the result of clinical negligence. The relevant principle was well explained in a Canadian case: *Montreal Tramways Co. v. Leveillé* (1933). A pregnant woman was thrown from a tram because of the motor man's negligence. As a result the baby was born with club feet and later successfully sued the tram company for damages. The operative principle as succinctly expressed by the Supreme Court of Canada is: "One may say that her right was born at the same time as she was." In other words, although the unborn child has no rights, its rights crystallize at birth, allowing it to bring claims relating even to the time when it was still in the womb. Another judge in the same case made an eloquent and impassioned appeal, pointing out that a denial of this right would leave the victim of prenatal injuries without a legal remedy: "To my mind it is but natural justice that a child, if born alive and viable, should be allowed to maintain an action in the Courts for injuries wrongfully committed upon its person in the womb of its mother."

No discussion of the rights of the unborn child can be considered complete without consideration of wills and inheritance. *Villar v. Gilbey* (1907) went all the way to the House of Lords on the meaning of the simple phrase "born in my lifetime". The claim was brought by a nephew of the deceased who was born just three weeks after his uncle's death. Did this entitle the nephew in question to be regarded as born in the testator's lifetime because he would certainly have been *en ventre sa mère* (in his mother's womb) at the time of his uncle's death? The House of Lords said No: "It is certain that a child *en ventre sa mère* is protected by the law, and may even be party to an action...but I do not think that it helps to establish a rule that the words 'born in my lifetime' include persons born some weeks or months later."

A Duty to Die

If you happen to be male, you can be called upon at any time to lay down your life for your country. In 1916, during that bloodiest and most avoidable war known as World War 1, the UK introduced conscription, or compulsory military service, for men aged between 18 and 41 the upper limit later being raised to 50 in the wake of the mass slaughter at the front. Needless to say, these lambs to the slaughter were never consulted. Conscription was simply introduced by legislation, the Military Service Act 1916. Many of the conscripts themselves did not even have the right to vote, which was only extended to all males over 21 (plus females aged over 30) with effect from 6 February 1918. The first general election since 1910 was held after the end of the war on 14 December 1918. By the time the war ended it is estimated that about 908,000 British (and Empire) troops had been killed, together with a further two million wounded. Not surprisingly, these men came to be known as "The Lost Generation".

The recruitment drive in World War 1 began with the famous poster showing Lord Kitchener, the Secretary of State for War, pointing out of the poster, with the words "Your

Country Needs YOU" in large letters. A less well-known but quite shameful poster published in 1915 showed a well-dressed mother and daughter haughtily observing a line of marching soldiers from a luxurious open window and calling out: "Women of Britain say – 'GO'!" while a frightened little boy looked on clinging to his mother's skirt. This poster was matched by the arrogance of women who accosted men in the street and ostentatiously presented them with a white feather, the badge of the coward, to shame them into joining up. Interestingly enough, this action was actively promoted by the dominant wing of the women's suffrage movement, or suffragettes, including Emmeline Pankhurst and her daughter Christabel, who were campaigning for women to be given the right to vote while also lobbying for compulsory conscription for mere males (which had not yet come in).

It never seemed to occur to these self-righteous and selfish women that maybe military service should be the price for the right to vote! Instead, these women just wanted special privileges for themselves – the same attitude that we find today among the "politically correct" with their emphasis on "equality" which really means "special privileges".

The white feather campaign was briefly renewed during World War 2, but conscription in that war did include single women aged between 20 and 30, though they were not assigned to front-line combat. National Service continued after the war until 1960 – but only for males aged between 17 and 21, who served for 18 months. Anti-male discrimination in regard to military service would be easy enough to justify in terms of anatomical, physiological and psychological differences between the sexes. But when it comes to differences between men and women in terms of interests, aptitude or intellect, politically correct accusations of unjust discrimination become increasingly shrill. [See Chapters 5 and 6].

A Right to Kill?
Convicted killers tend to be successful in the UK courts – not in their initial criminal trials but after conviction. Jury trials are the last vestige of democracy in the British legal system, although British juries do not have the same freedom as American juries, and British judges tend to exercise far too much control over the jury. Nevertheless, British juries generally have no problem convicting killers when presented with the evidence. However, after conviction, killers tend to start notching up court victories under human rights law. [See the Chapter on Fair Trials].

****

CHAPTER 4
Prohibition of Torture

Human rights claims generally have vertical effect, meaning that they are claims by individuals against the state or some other public authority. Human rights have occasionally been extended by the courts to have horizontal effect as well in cases between two individuals or entities neither of which is a public authority. [For more on this see Chapter 2]. But there is yet another highly disturbing extension of human rights law which is frequently applied by the courts in cases involving indirect allegations of torture. These are what might be called third-party cases, in which the UK Government is prevented by the courts from deporting terror suspects or convicted criminals on the ground that they might be subjected to torture if sent back to their home country. Not only does this amount to a baseless extension of the law, but it also represents an unwarranted encroachment by the judiciary on the preserve of the executive government preventing the government from carrying out its prime function of national security. Above all, the inordinate rights -- or really, privileges -- accorded to these terror suspects and convicted criminals are at the expense of the human rights of the vast majority of law-abiding and peace-loving citizens and other inhabitants of the UK, whose safety and security is endangered and who will generally have to finance the oft-repeated trips to court that these cases usually occasion.

The law in this area is governed by ECHR Article 3, the shortest of all the articles of the ECHR, which is also one of the few expressed in absolute terms without any restrictions or get-out clauses: *"No one shall be subjected to torture or to inhuman or degrading treatment or punishment."* Article 4 of the EU Charter has exactly the same wording. There are three degrees of forbidden treatment here, in descending order of seriousness:

(i) torture;
(ii) inhuman treatment or punishment;
(iii) degrading treatment or punishment.

The fact that "punishment" is specifically mentioned means that even judicial sentences are covered if deemed to be "inhuman" or "degrading".

The article therefore covers quite a wide range of activities, the test laid down by Strasbourg for the Article as a whole being that for any conduct to fall foul of the Article it must exceed "a certain roughness of treatment", a lamentably vague phrase. The guidelines were laid down in the interstate case of *Denmark, France, Norway, Sweden & the Netherlands v Greece*, commonly known as *The Greek Case* [(1969) 12 YB 1].

Torture
The only state actually found guilty of torture by the Strasbourg court is Turkey. A prime example is *Aydin v Turkey,* in which a Kurdish girl was found to have been

stripped, spun round in a car tyre, beaten, blindfolded and raped by village guards and police. By a majority of 14 to 7 the Strasbourg court found a violation of Article 3. Because of the cruel suffering caused by the rape this was classified as rape rather than as merely inhuman or degrading treatment. [(1998) 25 EHRR 251 97/71].

Al-Sweady Inquiry

Claims that British troops murdered, mutilated and tortured Iraqi detainees were found to be "wholly and entirely without merit or justification", according to the £31 million 1250-page five-year public Al-Sweady inquiry report published in December 2014. In the words of Sir Thayne Forbes, the chairman of the Inquiry: "I have come to the firm conclusion that the vast majority of the allegations made against the British military, which this Inquiry was required to investigate (including, without exception, all the most serious allegations), were wholly and entirely without merit or justification.

Very many of those baseless allegations were the product of deliberate and calculated lies on the part of those who made them and who then gave evidence to this inquiry in order to support and perpetuate them. Other false allegations were the result of inappropriate and reckless speculation on the part of witnesses......In contrast and except where otherwise expressly stated, for the most part I was generally impressed by the way in which the military witnesses approached the giving of their evidence to this

Inquiry......Except where otherwise expressly stated, in general I found the military witnesses to be both truthful and reliable." [Al-Sweady Executive Summary, ss.737ff.].

Inhuman Treatment and Punishment
Heczegfalvy v Austria (1993) explored the fine line between deliberate humiliation and bona fide medical treatment. Here a patient detained in a psychiatric institution claimed a violation of his rights under Articles 3, 5, 8, 10 and 13. He succeeded under Articles 5(4) and 10, but failed under the rest, including Article 3. In general, it was held, genuinely essential medical treatment could not be deemed inhuman or degrading, even if apparently cruel. The applicant had been force-fed and handcuffed to his bed for long periods. In the circumstances, however, it was held that this was justified for medical reasons, and no violation of Article 3 was found. [(1993) 15 EHRR 437 92/58].

Corporal Punishment
Several cases have been brought in Strasbourg against the UK in connection with corporal punishment. *Tyrer v United Kingdom* was a complaint by a 15-year-old boy who had been sentenced to three strokes of the birch by an Isle of Man court. The boy had to take down his trousers and underpants and bend over a table. The birching raised weals without actually breaking the skin and the boy was sore for about 10 days. By a majority of 6 to 1 the Strasbourg court found a violation of Article 3. [(1979-80) 2 EHRR 1 78/2]. The fact

that the caning was done on the boy's bare buttocks was seen as a factor contributing to the "degrading" nature of the punishment. The Isle of Man is a Crown possession and is not part of the United Kingdom but has its own laws, and by the time this case was heard corporal punishment had long been abandoned as a judicial sentence in the UK proper.

"Reasonable Chastisement"
There is a fine line between "reasonable chastisement" of children by their parents, which is still permissible, and assault, which is a crime.

See *A v UK* [1998] 2 FLR 959. A young boy complained that he had been beaten by his stepfather with a stick, causing bruising. The stepfather was acquitted by a jury of the charge of assault occasioning actual bodily harm, his defence being "reasonable chastisement". But the Strasbourg court held that the stepfather's action constituted "inhuman or degrading punishment" in violation of ECHR Article 3.

See also the booklet titled *Abolishing Corporal Punishment of Children*, published by the Council of Europe in 2007.

"Third-Party" Cases – Typical Scenario
These are now the commonest cases brought under ECHR Article 3 – cases in which the courts have prevented the government from deporting convicted criminals or terror suspects to their home countries on the ground that they may be subjected to torture there.

"Third-party" cases typically go through the following stages:

a) A convicted criminal or terror suspect is notified that the Home Secretary "deems his deportation to be conducive to the public good".
b) The person concerned is then detained pending his deportation.
c) The person concerned takes the matter to court claiming that if deported to his home country he will be likely to be tortured, in violation of his rights under ECHR Article 3.
d) The UK government obtains assurances from the person's home country that the person concerned will not be tortured if he is deported to that country.
e) Ignoring or rejecting such assurances, the court finds in favour of the applicant, preventing the UK government from deporting him.
f) In addition, as the person concerned cannot now be deported, he also cannot be detained as his detention was only meant to be "pending deportation".
g) So the person concerned wins and is allowed to remain in the UK.
h) The UK government loses and has egg all over its face.
i) But the real losers are justice and ordinary law-abiding UK citizens and other inhabitants, whose security is endangered by this decision and who as taxpayers will generally have to foot the bill for the legal to-ings and fro-ings and probably also for maintenance of the person concerned for an indefinite period.

Soering v. UK

This wrong approach to ECHR Article 3 started with the case of *Soering v. UK* [(1989) 11 EHRR 439]. Jens Soering, a German national living in the United States, brutally killed his girlfriend's parents, who had been opposed to his relationship with her. Their throats were slashed, the father was stabbed 39 times and the mother 8 times. [David Reed- www.apnewsarchive.com-25 June 1990]. Soering and his girlfriend, who was also involved in the murders, then fled to Britain, where they were arrested on charges of cheque fraud. Soon after this Soering was indicted with the capital murder of his girlfriend's parents. The United States requested Soering's extradition under the 1972 extradition treaty between the two countries and a warrant was duly issued under the Extradition Act 1870 to commit him to prison to await the Home Secretary's order to extradite him to the US. Soering's appeal to the House of Lords (then the highest law court) and his petition to the Home Secretary both failed. The case then went to the European Commission of Human Rights, which decided that extradition would not constitute inhuman or degrading treatment contrary to ECHR Article 3. However, the Strasbourg court itself ruled in favour of Soering on the ground that the "death row phenomenon" breached Article 3, the relevant factors being essentially the length of time he was likely to have to spend on "death row" prior to his execution, and the conditions on death row: "Having regard to the very long period of time spent on death row in such extreme conditions, with the ever present and mounting anguish of awaiting execution of the death penalty, and to the personal circumstances of the applicant, especially his age and mental state at the time of the offence, the applicant's extradition to the United States would expose him to a real risk of treatment going beyond the threshold set by Article 3." After obtaining assurances from the US that the state of Virginia would not seek the death penalty against Soering, the UK extradited Soering to Virginia. At his trial, his girlfriend, who had pleaded guilty, testified that Soering had committed the murders and that she had been an accessory. Soering was convicted on two counts of first degree murder and on 4 September 1990 was sentenced to two consecutive life terms. His repeated applications for early release, ending up in the US Supreme Court, have all been turned down.

The same approach to ECHR Article 3 was applied by Strasbourg in *Chahal v. UK* [1996] ECHR 54, which has been followed on numerous occasions by the UK courts. [See Chapter 1].

Main Objections

The main objections to this interpretation of ECHR Article 3 are:

a) Why should the UK be responsible for the way a foreign country treats someone who is rightly being removed from the UK?

b) In Soering's case, why should he have been given special privileges not enjoyed by other murderers in the state of Virginia?

c) And Soering was only in the UK as a fugitive from justice in the US.
d) Moreover, it is a complete misinterpretation of Article 3 to oblige country X to force country Y to adopt the standards of country X.
e) And ECHR Article 1 makes it absolutely crystal clear that the obligations of the signatory states, including the UK, in regard to the ECHR apply only within their own jurisdictions. [See more on this below].
f) Above all, the UK courts are not obliged to follow Strasbourg slavishly, as they tend to do. Section 2(1)(a) of the Human Rights Act only requires them to "take into account" judgments, decisions, declarations etc. of the Strasbourg court. [See Michael Arnheim, The Problem with Human Rights Law, Civitas, 2015].

Saadi v. Italy (2008) – the UK's brief moment of defiance

The most extreme example of this "politically correct" approach on the part of the Strasbourg court was reached in the case of Nassim Saadi against Italy, in which the UK actually had the gumption to intervene as a third party to try to persuade the Strasbourg court to give up their irrational approach. Saadi, a Tunisian national legally resident in Italy, was arrested as a terrorist suspect in 2002. After a lengthy process, involving several appeals, he was released in 2006. In the meantime he was convicted in Tunisia of terrorist offences and sentenced to 20 years' imprisonment. Saadi was then served by the Italian government with a deportation order. Saadi then played the "Torture Card", applying for political asylum in Italy on the ground that he would be at risk of torture if returned to Tunisia. His asylum application was denied on the grounds of national security and Italy received assurances from Tunisia that Saadi would not be tortured if deported to Tunisia.

The UK as an "intervener" actually put some cogent arguments backing up the Italian Government's attempt to deport the terrorist suspect. [*Saadi v Italy* 37201/06, 28 February 2008]. The UK government's sensible and logical arguments included the following:

- The degree of danger posed by the applicant should be taken into account – contrary to a supposed principle laid down by the Strasbourg court in *Chahal v UK* (1996) 23 EHRR 413.
- The "real risk of torture or ill-treatment" standard laid down in *Chahal* should be modified and clarified in two respects. First, the security risk posed by the applicant's dangerousness should be weighed against the risk to the applicant in the receiving state.
- And secondly, the standard applicable to a terror suspect should be that he is "more likely than not" to be exposed to prohibited treatment rather than the lower "real risk" standard currently applied.

Although the Strasbourg court accepted the right of member states like the UK and Italy to control the entry, residence and expulsion of aliens and confirmed that there is no Convention right to political asylum, it reasserted its longstanding insistence on the absolute nature of Article 3.

A few years later, the Strasbourg court actually softened its position in a more reasonable direction in *Babar Ahmad and Abu Hamza Othman v. UK* [2012] ECHR 609: "The absolute nature of Article 3 does not mean that any form of ill treatment will act as a bar to removal from a Contracting State....this court has repeatedly stated that the convention does not purport to be a means of requiring the contracting states to impose convention standards on other states....This being so, treatment which might violate Article 3 because of an act or omission of a contracting state might not attain the minimum level of severity which is required for there to be a violation of Article 3 in an expulsion or extradition case" [at §177].

A Recent "Third-Party" Case

However, the English courts have not always been so flexible. In a recent "third-party" case finally decided in April 2016, six unnamed Algerian terror suspects with alleged links to al-Qaeda won a ten-year deportation battle against the British Government and were effectively granted the right to live in Britain. The Government admitted defeat and announced that they would not be appealing against this decision handed down by the Special Immigration Appeals Commission (SIAC). The trump card played by the six terror suspects was the "torture card", an allegation that if deported to Algeria they would be at risk of torture. The court agreed with the terror suspects, concluding: "It is not inconceivable that these Appellants, if returned to Algeria, would be subjected to ill-treatment infringing Article 3 [of the ECHR]. There is a real risk of such a breach." To protect the identity of the terror suspects, the case is reported only as *BB, PP, W, U, Y & Z v Secretary of State for the Home Department* [SC/39/2005, 18 April 2016]. A Home Office spokesman made this lame comment: "We are extremely disappointed with SIAC's judgment. Our priority remains the safety and protection of the British public and we will continue to take every measure possible to remove foreign nationals who we deem a risk." [Robert Mendick, "Judges stop Theresa May deporting terror suspects". *The Telegraph*, 7 May 2016: lack of a robust system of verification.]

This is a really troubling decision – and no less so for being just the latest in a long list of similar decisions. Here are some of the major issues raised by this decision:

- This decision was *not* made by any European court but by a domestic UK court. Brexit will not improve matters in this respect.
- You may perhaps be thinking: "This decision does seem a bit over-the-top, but what harm can it do to be kind?" In fact, it Can do a lot of harm – even to you personally. Having potentially dangerous people on the loose threatens your personal safety. If allowed to remain in Britain, such people may possibly be

subjected to supposedly strict conditions – which however are never as secure as they are meant to be and which will be financed at great cost by you as a taxpayer.

- These applicants are protected by anonymity – why? It is only terror suspects and convicted criminals, including convicted killers, who can expect this kind of privilege – because that is what it is, not a right but a special privilege.
- But why should people who are a potential danger to society be accorded this privilege when their potential victims -- like yourself -- would be laughed out of court if they tried to apply for the same protection?
- For that matter, how did these people get into Britain in the first place? It appears that they were given political asylum by the UK government -- even though terror suspects -- are disqualified from applying for asylum under Article 1F or Article 33(2) of the Refugee Convention and Art 14(5) of the Qualification Directive.
- [See Home Office booklet: "Exclusion (Article 1F) and Article 33(2) of the Refugee Convention", version 6 1 July 2016].
- Government's dereliction of duty: The six terror suspects in this particular case came from Algeria, a non-EU country with no connection with the UK. Their entry into Britain can only be blamed on the UK

Government's dismal failure over many years to control immigration from *outside* the EU.

But, all that aside, what is wrong with SIAC's decision to block their deportation back to Algeria?

- You just need to read the SIAC court ruling to see on what a flimsy and insubstantial legal foundation it rests: "It is not inconceivable that these Appellants, if returned to Algeria, would be subjected to ill-treatment infringing Article 3 [of the ECHR]. There is a real risk of such a breach." "*Not inconceivable*" and "*real risk*"? Is that all? What exactly is "a real risk" anyway? A 10% risk, a 25% risk, or what? It's *not* a 50% risk – as we know from the fact that the much fairer test of "more likely than not" proposed by the UK Government was dismissed out of hand by the Strasbourg court in *Saadi v Italy* in 2008.
- Besides the use of the vague phrases "not inconceivable" and "real risk", SIAC does not even go so far as to say that there was a risk of *torture*, but only the much weaker risk of "ill-treatment infringing Article 3".
- In the forlorn hope of being able to persuade "politically correct" judges to allow it to deport terror suspects and convicted criminals -- a right that belongs to any sovereign state -- the British Government has systematically compiled elaborate documentation in

support of a policy of *deportation with assurances* (DWA). This entailed obtaining assurances from the governments of countries to which the UK Government wished to order deportations. One of these countries was Algeria – and the British Government in fact received personal assurances about these individual cases from the Algerian President.

- But even this was not good enough for SIAC, who concluded: "The different means of verification of adherence advanced by the Respondent [the UK Government] do not, taken together, amount to a robust system of verification."
- But why should it be the UK Government's responsibility to provide "a robust system of verification"-- or any system of verification -- anyway?
- In short, why should Britain be responsible for what happens to someone who shouldn't be in the UK in the first place?
- This is a complete misinterpretation of ECHR Article 3. All that ECHR Article 3 says is: *"No one shall be subjected to torture or to inhuman or degrading treatment or punishment."*
- The courts are keen to stress the "absolute" nature of this Article – the absence of any exceptions. But ALL the human rights of the ECHR are governed by ECHR Article 1, which reads: *"The High Contracting Parties shall secure to everyone within their jurisdiction the*

rights and freedoms defined in Section 1 of this Convention." The term "the High Contracting Parties" refers to the governments of all signatories of the ECHR, including the UK Government. But the really significant phrase here is **"within their jurisdiction"**. What this means as far as ECHR Article 3 is concerned is that the UK's responsibility for protecting people against torture and inhuman treatment does not extend to beyond the areas under UK Government control.

- In *Al-Skeini v UK* [Application 55721/07], decided in 2011, 'the Strasbourg court itself, in its most extended interpretation of ECHR Article 1 to date, still restricted the UK's human rights responsibilities to areas directly controlled by the UK Government. The case involved six Iraqi civilians killed by British troops in Basrah, in Iraq. The complaint was not of any substantive breach of the right to life under ECHR Article 2, but only that the UK Government had not carried out an effective investigation into the killings. Between the removal of Sadam Hussain and the appointment of an interim Iraqi Government, the court held, "the United Kingdom (together with the United States) assumed in Iraq the exercise of some of the public powers normally to be exercised by a sovereign government....In these exceptional circumstances, the Court considers that the United Kingdom, through its soldiers engaged in security operations in Basrah during the period in question, exercised authority and control over individuals killed in the course of such security operations, so as to establish a jurisdictional link between the deceased and the United Kingdom for the purposes of Article 1 of the Convention." [§149]. So, even in these *"exceptional circumstances"* it was only because the UK *"exercised authority and control"* so as to establish *"a jurisdictional link"* that the UK was held by Strasbourg to have had any human rights responsibilities.

- This only underlines just how wrong it is to make the UK Government responsible for what happens to terror suspects in Algeria -- a country over which the UK exercises no control of any kind -- to the point of preventing the UK Government from keeping its people safe, the prime duty of any government.
- It is important to note in regard to the Algerian terror-suspects case, that, while SIAC, a domestic UK court, has stuck to the old hard-line Strasbourg approach -- which it did not have to do -- Strasbourg itself has in the meantime softened its position in these "third-party" Article 3 cases. For example, in a case involving extradition from the UK to the USA of four applicants, whose attempt to use the "torture trump" card -- amazingly -- failed on this occasion. A unanimous Strasbourg court waved the four men off to their new American home without so much as a tear, holding that if the four men were extradited to the USA, "there

would be no violation of Article 3 of the Convention as a result of the length of their possible sentences" or "as a result of conditions at ADX Florence [a maximum security US federal penitentiary in Colorado]." *(Babar Ahmad & Abu Hamza (Othman) v UK* [2012] ECHR 609). "The absolute nature of Article 3 does not mean that any form of ill treatment will act as a bar to removal from a Contracting State......This court has repeatedly stated that the Convention does not purport to be a means of requiring the contracting states to impose convention standards on other states....This being so, treatment which might violate Article 3 because of an act or omission of a contracting state might not attain the minimum level of severity which is required for there to be a violation of Article 3 in an expulsion or extradition case."[§177].

What can be done to counter this kind of decision?
Parliament can override the decision by passing an Act of Parliament. Shock, horror! Most people don't know about this power. It is an integral part of the Sovereignty of Parliament, the bedrock principle of the UK constitution. It also ties in with the checks and balances which form an integral part of the doctrine of the separation of powers, which is negated if, as is the case at present, the other two branches of government, namely the legislature and the executive, abdicate their own responsibilities and kowtow to the judiciary.

The best example of Parliament's exercise of this power occurred in the case of *Burmah Oil v. Lord Advocate* [1965] AC 75, in which the House of Lords as the top court decided by a 3-2 majority that the British Government should compensate an oil company for destroying oil fields during World War 2. The majority really went to town with extremely wordy opinions which purported to lay down some fundamental constitutional principles. But the House of Lords decision in *Burmah Oil* was soon reversed by the War Damage Act 1965, which was not only an act of Parliament but also one with retroactive effect. (Strangely enough, it was cited by the UK Supreme Court in its Brexit decision in 2017, without any mention of the fact that the House of Lords' decision in *Burmah Oil* had been overridden by an Act of Parliament).

Bejhaj v. Straw (2017)

The *Burmah Oil* court decision was not nearly as damaging to national security as some recent court decisions, like, for example, the BB case itself and *Belhaj v. Straw* [2017] UKSC 3. This was a claim for compensation by a Libyan national, a political opponent of the Gaddafi regime, and his Moroccan wife. They fled from Libya to China intending to claim asylum in the UK, but when on a commercial flight bound for London via Bangkok, they were taken off the aircraft in Bangkok by Thai officials and delivered to agents of the United States. They were then flown to Libya in a US-registered aircraft, where they were taken to Tajoura prison. The claimant's wife was released in June 2004 after being held there for more than three months. Abdul-Hakim Belhaj himself was held in Libyan prisons for six years before being released in March 2010. "It is alleged that they were tortured and subjected to other serious mistreatment by US officials in Bangkok and in the aircraft carrying them to Libya, and by Libyan officials in Libya....The present proceedings are brought in support of a claim for damages against a number of departments and officials of the British government who are said to have been complicit in what happened to them.....It is not alleged that British officials were directly involved in the rendition, torture or mistreatment of the claimants. But it is said that they enabled it to happen, knowing of the risk that the defendants would be unlawfully detained, tortured and otherwise mistreated by the Americans and the Libyans. It is also alleged that British officials took advantage of Mr Belhaj's detention in Libya by interrogating him there at least twice. The defendants, it is said, thereby incurred liability in tort." [*Belhaj v. Straw* [2017 UKSC 3, *per* Lord Sumption]. The UK's alleged involvement in the alleged torture, inhumane and degrading treatment was therefore extremely remote, if it occurred at all. No proof of these allegations was presented, and even the UK Supreme Court accepted the first instance judge's finding "that all the claims depend upon proof that torts such as those alleged existed under the laws of the places where they were allegedly committed...."

In a sensible and carefully argued judgment in the High Court, the judge, Simon J, therefore struck out the claims against the

UK for "unlawful rendition" on the basis that the doctrine of immunity attaching to an "act of state" is a total bar to such claims, regardless of their gravity. [*Belhaj v. Straw* [2013] EWHC 411 (QB). See Rosalind English, "Rendition to Libya an 'act of state' and therefore non-justiciable". ukhumanrightsblog.com – 14 January 2014].

The "Act of State" doctrine obliges every sovereign state to respect the independence of every other sovereign state, so that the courts of one state will not sit in judgment on the acts of another state's government. It was on this basis that the judge came to the conclusion that the UK government was right in submitting "that the case pleaded against them depends on the Court having to decide that the conduct of US officials acting outside the United States was unlawful, in circumstances where there are no clear and incontrovertible standards for doing so and where there is incontestable evidence that such an enquiry would be damaging to the national interest. The most recent and authoritative decision, *Rahmatullah*, makes clear....that this is something that the domestic court should not do." [*Belhaj v. Straw* [2013] EWHC 411 (QB)].

This careful and sensible judgment was reversed by the Court of Appeal and, for different reasons, by the UK Supreme Court, where the justices took a different view of the meaning of "act of state" from the judge and even, to some extent, from one another. This case, in an area where the relevant law is unclear and which threatens national security, cries out for the intervention of Parliament. Unfortunately, there is no possibility that the current government of Theresa May will heed this warning. We can only hope that there will come a time in the not-too-distant future when the UK will have a proper government.

****

CHAPTER 5
Your Right To Freedom of Expression

What are the limits of freedom of expression? Do you have the right to shout "Fire!" in a crowded theatre when there is no fire? Do you have the right to attack someone in print or on the internet? And what rights do you have against someone who attacks you in print or on the internet? How does individual freedom of expression relate to press freedom? And, above all, what happens when there is a clash between freedom of expression and some other right, like privacy? These questions are answered below, and the last one in the next chapter.

If you thought you were going to be able to celebrate your much-touted right to freedom of expression, I am sorry to disappoint you, because freedom of expression is one of many areas where your rights have actually shrunk. Sure, you can mount your soapbox in Speaker's Corner in London's Hyde Park and shout your lungs out, but you will be drowned out by an opponent with a megaphone or a bullhorn, not to mention by a loudspeaker blaring from the top of a passing speakervan. The internet is open to all, but unless you have millions of followers on social media, you will not be able to compete with the media moguls.

The irony therefore is that, now that there is greater access to the airwaves than ever before, there is also a greater disparity between the *degrees* of access enjoyed by different people. Your freedom of expression will depend to a large extent on the degree of access available to you. True freedom of expression will depend on equality of access, which does not exist. On the contrary, as time goes by, the inequality of different people's access to the airwaves increases.

And the same applies to the written word. Again, anybody can have a website of their own, but driving traffic to that website will cost time, money and effort. Competing with the big boys is not easy. Once again, it is a question of equality. Two hundred years ago, anyone with a hand-operated printing press in their backroom could compete with the major publishers. No longer. You can write the proverbial great British novel, but unless you can interest a major publisher your book will probably never see the light of day, and even then is unlikely ever to hit the bookshops, most of which are in the hands of a worryingly small number of players.

Libel

One of the main constraints on freedom of expression is the law of defamation, a combination of libel (for anything in permanent form) and slander (for live speech). English libel law traditionally favoured claimants, even in cases of supposedly unwitting defamation, as in an old case where a journalist who wrote about an unsavoury but supposedly fictitious character called Artemus Jones was successfully sued by a real Artemus Jones. The novelist Jilly Cooper was similarly threatened with a defamation action on the basis that her fictitious nasty boss of Cotswold Television, Lord Bullingdon, bore too close a resemblance to the Mr Bullingham who was an actual former director of Cotswold Cable Television – both men also being Rottweiler owners! Also, what is considered defamatory at one time may be regarded as positively flattering at another. So, in *Tolley v. Fry* [1931] AC 333 a well-known golfer successfully sued the makers of a chocolate bar for showing the golfer commending the chocolate in an advertisement. The defamation consisted in the fact that the advertisement gave the impression that the golfer had been paid to promote the chocolate, thus besmirching his proud amateur status! Perhaps the most sensational case of this kind was *Liberace v. Daily Mirror* (1959), in which the well-known flamboyant American entertainer, Liberace, successfully sued a newspaper over an article strongly suggesting that he was gay. Male homosexuality was illegal in Britain at the time.

Most but by no means all libel cases are brought against the media. One notable exception was the so-called "McLibel case" brought by McDonalds, the hamburger chain, against two environmental activists who had published a leaflet critical of McDonalds: *McDonalds v. Steel and Morris* [1997] EWHC QB 366. After a ten-year legal tussle McDonalds won and were awarded £40,000, which they announced that they did not plan to collect. The losing defendants then took the case to Strasbourg, where they won against the UK on the ground that there had been a violation of their rights under both Article 10 (freedom of expression) and Article 6 (fair trial), the latter largely because legal aid was not available in defamation cases: *Steel and Morris v. UK* [2005] ECHR 103.

English libel law was long criticized for encouraging "libel tourism", attracting foreign claimants to file suit in England rather than in the jurisdiction with which the case was more closely connected. In reaction to this the Defamation Act 2013 was passed, which favours the media in a number of respects. For one thing, a claimant now has to show actual or probable serious harm. In addition, the law also swept away the presumption of jury trial in defamation cases, thus also benefiting the media, as a jury is more likely than a judge to favour victims of the press over the media moguls.

The leading libel judge from 1997 to 2013, Sir David Eady, was criticized for having "delivered a series of rulings that have bolstered privacy laws and encouraged libel tourism". [*The Times*, 7 June 2009]. Paul Dacre, editor of the *Daily Mail*, described Eady J as having been "given a virtual monopoly of all cases against the media, enabling him to bring in a privacy law by the back door". [*The Guardian*, 9 December 2009]. In *Max Mosley v. News Group Newspapers* [2008] EWHC 177 (QB), Eady awarded £60,000 to Max Mosley, a leading figure in motor sport who also happened to be the son of the British Fascist leader, Sir Oswald Mosley, for invasion of privacy. [For more on this see Chapter 6]. Eady also issued a number of "super-injunctions" to (usually anonymous) sportsmen and other "celebrities" preventing publication of embarrassing details of their private lives.

An important decision by Eady J was his 2009 ruling that Google was not liable for defamatory comments in news articles, blogs and forums that came up in a Google search: *Metropolitan International Schools v. Google* [2009] EWHC 1765 (QB). Google's position was that it was not responsible for the allegedly defamatory words or comments. The judge agreed: "Google has merely, by the provision of its search service, played the role of a facilitator." The law in this area is now bedevilled by inconsistent Strasbourg decisions.

Offensive Comments on the Internet

In 2015 the Strasbourg court ruled that a Hungarian online news portal could not be held responsible for offensive or vulgar comments posted anonymously by its readers. (*MTE-Index v. Hungary* [2016] ECHR 135). The operators of the website had been held liable by the Hungarian courts for reader comments. This was held by Strasbourg to have violated the website operators' right to freedom of expression under ECHR Article 10.

Shortly before this decision, another similar case had had a completely opposite outcome before the Strasbourg court. This was a case called *Delfi v. Estonia* [(2015) ECHR 6469/09], involving a popular Estonian online news portal which had published a number of comments which could be classified as hate speech and some which had even incited violence against a particular individual. In this case by a 15-2 majority Strasbourg held that the Estonian courts had not violated the portal operators' Article 10 rights by holding them liable for the offensive posts. The outcome in this case came as something of a surprise, especially in the light of the EU's E-Commerce Directive, Article 14 of which lays down an "actual knowledge" standard. The main difference between the two cases is that the Estonian case involved hate speech and incitements to violence against an individual, while the Hungarian case was concerned only with offensive speech against a commercial company.

Political Correctness and Free Speech

Undoubtedly the biggest constraint on freedom of expression today is "political correctness", which has developed into an ethos with a stranglehold over the chattering classes in the West.

Shouting "Fire"

In the United States, unlike the UK, there is no "hate speech" exception to the right of freedom of expression. In the words of UCLA law professor Eugene Volokh: "[T]here is no hate speech exception to the First Amendment....One is as free to condemn Islam – or Muslims, or Jews, or blacks, or whites, or illegal aliens – as one is to condemn capitalism or Socialism or Democrats or Republicans." [*Washington Post*, May 7, 2015]. However, that is not to say that there are no legally recognized exceptions to the First Amendment right of freedom of speech. A well known exception -- which applies in the UK as well -- is shouting "Fire" in a crowded theatre when there is no fire. This is based on a much-overused dictum by Justice Oliver Wendell Holmes Jr in the case of *Schenck v. U.S.* (1919): "The most stringent protection of free speech would not protect a man in falsely shouting fire in a theatre and causing panic." The case concerned a pamphlet written by Charles Schenck and Elizabeth Baer, leading Socialists, calling upon men drafted into the army in World War I to resist induction: "Do not submit to intimidation -- Assert your rights". The pamphlet suggested that conscription constituted involuntary servitude or a form of slavery, which was prohibited by the Thirteenth Amendment. After being convicted in separate jury trials under the Espionage Act of 1917, Schenck and Baer appealed to the U.S. Supreme Court on the ground that their convictions and indeed the Espionage Act itself were unconstitutional, being contrary to the First Amendment. Schenck and Baer lost their appeal.

In the words of Oliver Wendell Holmes Jr., who wrote the Court's unanimous opinion: "The question in every case is whether the words used are....of such a nature as to create a clear and present danger that they will bring about the substantive evils that Congress has a right to prevent."

In *Abrams v. U.S.*, another American case concerning the Espionage Act of 1917, and decided just a few days after *Schenck*, Oliver Wendell Holmes adopted a more liberal position and indignantly dissented, on the ground that Abrams and his fellow anarchists lacked the "specific intent" to obstruct the war effort. The prosecution of Abrams and his friends, said Holmes, amounted to an outrageous abuse of power on the part of the government. Trying to suppress opinions by force, he held, contradicted the First Amendment, which required instead "free trade in ideas": "The best test of truth is the power of the thought to get itself accepted in the competition of the market, and that truth is the only ground upon which their wishes safely can be carried out."

Holmes's rather naïve dissenting opinion in *Abrams* muddied the waters. The "clear and present danger" test proposed by Holmes in *Schenck* was eventually replaced by a test of "imminent lawless action" approved by a unanimous U.S. Supreme Court in *Brandenburg v. Ohio* (1968). This was a most unlikely case to attract the protection of free speech. Clarence Brandenburg, a leading Ku Klux Klan member, announced plans for a march on Washington. Convicted of "advocating violence", he eventually appealed to the U.S. Supreme Court on the ground that his conviction violated his First Amendment and Fourteenth Amendment right to freedom of speech. He won. The majority opinion held that "the constitutional guarantees of free speech and free press do not permit a State to forbid or proscribe advocacy of the use of force or of law violation except where such advocacy is directed to inciting or producing imminent lawless action and is likely to incite or produce such action".

This decision made it very difficult to prosecute someone for mere threatening words.

Public Order Act 1986

So, could you be prosecuted in the UK for shouting "Fire" in a crowded theatre? Probably. It is likely to fall under the general heading of "hate speech" law, which has no real parallel in US law. A celebrated English case involved Harry Hammond, a street evangelist who was prosecuted in 2002 under section 5 of the Public Order Act 1986. Harry Hammond preached Christianity while holding up a sign reading: "Jesus Gives Peace, Jesus is Alive", and on the reverse side: "Stop Immorality, Stop Homosexuality, Stop Lesbianism, Jesus is Lord." A group of 30 to 40 young people gathered around, arguing and shouting, and the preacher was assailed with water and soil. No one in the crowd was arrested, but Harry Hammond was charged under section 5 of the Public Order Act 1986, which at the time provided that:

"A person is guilty of an offence if he....displays any writing, sign or other visible representation which is threatening, abusive or insulting, within the hearing or sight of a person likely to be caused harassment, alarm or distress thereby.....It is a defence for the accused to prove that his conduct was reasonable." Harry Hammond was convicted by a magistrates' court and ordered to pay a fine of £300 and costs of £395. The offending signs were ordered to be destroyed, but the preacher died shortly afterwards. A posthumous appeal to the Court of Appeal, based on ECHR Article 10 (right to freedom of expression), was unsuccessful on the ground that the magistrates' court had not been wrong to find "that the words displayed on the sign were insulting" and that the preacher's conduct had not been reasonable either under ECHR Article 10 or under ECHR Article 9 (freedom of religion). [*Hammond v. Department of Public Prosecutions* [2004] EWHC 69 (Admin)]. The word "insulting" was actually deleted from section 5 of the 1986 Act in 2013. Would this have made any difference to the outcome of the Hammond case? Probably not, because his placard would very likely still have been found to have been "abusive".

Public Nudity

The other limb of section 5 of the Public Order Act 1986 lumps words and conduct together: "A person is guilty of an offence if he – uses threatening or abusive words or behaviour, or disorderly behaviour….within the hearing or sight of a person likely to be caused harassment, alarm or distress thereby." I am glad to say that in 2012 I was successful in obtaining the acquittal of a client of mine who had been convicted under this subsection for rambling naked in broad daylight in a quiet part of the Yorkshire countryside and allegedly "causing distress" to an unnamed female dog walker, who was not called to give evidence. I had not represented the naked rambler at first instance, but only in the appeal to the Crown Court, where the judge held that my client did not have a sexual motive for his conduct: "He was not deliberately flaunting himself or seeking attention or jumping out and doing what is colloquially called 'flashing'". And: "In view of the location of this incident, the time of day and the reaction of others as we have found it to be, we do not consider that anyone was likely to be harassed by this behaviour or intimidated or distressed."

"Hate Speech"

The UK Race Relations Act 1976 is a good example, forbidding speech "that expresses racial hatred not only when it is likely to lead to violence, but generally, on the ground that members of minority races should be protected from racial insults." How does this prohibition gel with the right to freedom of speech enshrined in ECHR Article 10 incorporated into the UK Human Rights Act 1998? The answer is that there is a complete clash here between two beliefs: the belief in free speech and the belief in non-discrimination – both of which are championed by the PC brigade! Needless to say, victory will generally go to non-discrimination morphing into special privilege. Not even a troubled child can be allowed any latitude.

In *Sheffield City Council v. Norouzi* [UKEAT/0497/10/RN] an Iranian residential social worker at a home for troubled children complained of harassment and indirect racial discrimination at the hands of a girl aged between 11 and 15 who "was often abusive and offensive" to the claimant "on racial grounds" and who "mocked and mimicked his accent". An Employment Tribunal held that the Council had not done enough to protect the claimant from the alleged harassment and discrimination by the child and was therefore liable for racial harassment and racial discrimination. This decision was upheld by the Employment Appeal Tribunal. One comment by the judge was: "To mock a racial characteristic seems to us plainly analogous with overtly racial abuse." What was the Council supposed to do – discipline the troubled child? That could have caused even more trouble. And how in any event can a non-discriminatory attitude be inculcated into a child? By the singing of Kumbaya around a campfire? Of course, the suggestion that a grown-up professional social worker should know how to deal with childish taunts would obviously not be acceptable in the PC world of modern Britain.

PC Origins

"Political correctness" (PC) started as a faintly comical ban on language perceived as insulting to minority groups of various kinds. Hence "vertically challenged" for short; "sex worker" for prostitute; and "undocumented immigrant" for illegal alien, "developing countries" for *third world*, and of course "gay" for *homosexual* and now "transgender" or just "trans" for *sex-change*.

Some PC words -- like "Native American" for American Indian -- while purportedly protecting a threatened minority, are insulting to the majority: for "Native American" is a description which rightfully belongs to anyone born in America (however defined), regardless of ethnicity.

The "N-word" was one of the first to become a taboo word, being replaced by "colored" or "black" and now mainly by "African-American". So toxic has the "N-word" become that even words that sound similar but are completely unrelated to it are banned as well. Among these is the word *niggardly*, which is related to *niggle* and to the common German word *genau*, meaning "precise, exact".

Other race-related terms have also come under fire. "Inuit" (literally, "the people") has come to replace *Eskimo,* although the Yupik people of Alaska do not accept the "Inuit" label, still preferring "Eskimo". And some PC words like ["Native American" for *American Indian*] while purportedly protecting a threatened minority, are insulting to the majority: for "Native American" is a description which rightfully belongs to *anyone* born in America (however defined), regardless of ethnicity. ("Indian" is of course itself a misnomer, as it derives from the mistake made by Christopher Columbus in thinking he had landed in India when he hit Central America!).

No PC issues are more emotionally charged than those concerning gender. Words ending in "-man" have been reformulated with "-person" or some other gender-neutral suffix, as in "chairperson" for *chairman,* "firefighter" for *fireman,* and, as was recently announced by the US Marines, "basic infantry Marine" for *basic infantryman.* Similarly, a female actor is no longer an *actress* but an "actor" and a female poet is just a "poet", not a *poetess.* Female Representatives elected to the US Congress appear to buck this trend, with the majority still referring to themselves as *Congresswoman,* a few as *Congressman* and a few others simply as *Representative.*

The search for gender-neutral language may result in resorting to some awkward circumlocutions. "A student's mastery of grammar may impress *his* teacher" is replaced by "A student's mastery of grammar may impress *his or her* teacher" or "A student's mastery of grammar may impress *their* teacher". And there is now great pressure, especially in universities, to use gender-neutral pronouns when referring to someone who does not wish to be described as either "he" or "she". [See below].

Another aspect of the feminist influence on language is women's desire to copy men in not being defined by their marital status. Hence the increasing use of "Ms" or "Ms." as a universal honorific for all women whether single or married and replacing both "Miss" and "Mrs". A further step in the same direction is the growing trend for a married woman to retain her maiden name instead of taking her husband's last name, or for both spouses to combine both names in a double-barrelled name, or at least for the wife to use her maiden name as a middle name, as in: Hillary Rodham Clinton.

Non-PC French, German and Spanish

It is worth mentioning that gender-neutral language is a feature of the English language which does not carry over to other languages such as French or German. So, in German Angela Merkel cannot be described as *Bundeskanzler* (Federal Chancellor) but has to be described by the specifically feminine *Bundeskanzlerin* (literally, "Federal Chancelloress"). In French, similarly, Marine Le Pen is *la présidente* (not *le président*) of the National Front party, a title which at the time of writing she is hoping to replicate in regard to France as a whole.

In Spanish, the late Cuban dictator known as Fidel Castro was actually Fidel Castro Ruz, Ruz being his mother's maiden name. This has nothing to do with Castro's left-wing politics. It is standard – and very traditional – nomenclature throughout the Spanish-speaking world. Similarly, the former Spanish dictator Francisco Franco was Francisco Franco Bahamonde, Bahamonde again being his mother's maiden name.

PC Shows its Claws
These linguistic features of French, German and Spanish have no relevance to the presence or absence of PC.

But PC language in the English-speaking world soon revealed its claws, showing that it is actually prepared to attempt to force people to obey its dictates. In the UK, section 18 of the Public Order Act 1986 provides that: *A person who uses threatening, abusive or insulting words or behaviour, or displays any written material which is threatening, abusive or insulting, is guilty of an offence if – (a) he intends thereby to stir up racial hatred, or (b) having regard to all the circumstances racial hatred is likely to be stirred up thereby.*

This provision is alarmingly broad. To constitute a crime the offending words, behaviour or writing do not even have to reach the level of threats or abuse. Insults are enough. The offending speech, behaviour or writing do have to make racial hatred "likely to be stirred up", but what exactly does that mean? The legislation is deliberately worded so as not to depend on the intention of the offender. It's enough if his words or conduct make it "likely" that racial hatred is "stirred up" – a vague term which has no place in legislation.

What is the purpose of this harsh and punitive legislation? It is no doubt motivated by the desire to protect ethnic minorities, but it contains within itself a tacit recognition that the use of racial "hate speech" by one person may "stir up" others to follow suit. This amounts to a tacit admission that the liberal purpose of the legislation is probably not shared by the populace at large. Otherwise, the use of racial "hate speech" by one person might have been expected to elicit a hostile reaction from those hearing it, coming to the defence of the racial minority against which it was aimed. And does this kind of legislation not fly directly in the face of the right to freedom of speech, as enshrined in Article 10 of the European Convention of Human Rights?

Academic Freedom

Universities, supposed bastions of free speech, are one of the key battlegrounds over PC speech. The serious 2005 incident involving President Larry Summers of Harvard, a distinguished liberal economist, is one of the most shocking examples of PC victimization, but by no means the only one. At a national conference on "Diversifying the Science & Engineering Workforce", Summers gingerly broached the question of why women were underrepresented "in tenured positions in science and engineering at top universities and research institutions". He offered three alternative explanations for this, one of which was that proportionally more boys than girls tended to score very high (and also very low) in high-school Maths tests. This very cautious remark, based on detailed statistical evidence, was enough to cause a firestorm. Summers was immediately accused of sexism and even of careless scholarship.

Was it wrong to suggest that the different levels of achievement between males and females in maths and science could possibly be explained by genetics or biology? Not at all. When asked whether Summers' talk was "within the pale of legitimate academic discourse", Professor Steven Pinker, a well respected Harvard psychologist, commented: "Good grief, shouldn't everything be within the pale of legitimate academic discourse, as long as it is presented with some degree of rigor? That's the difference between a university and a madrassa. There is certainly enough evidence for the hypothesis to be taken seriously." [Steven Pinker: "Psychoanalysis Q-and-A", *The Harvard Crimson*, January 19, 2005].

Despite repeated apologies by Summers, his critics remained implacable. The Harvard Faculty of Arts and Sciences passed a motion of "lack of confidence" in his leadership by 218 votes to 185. Harvard students were more supportive. In one poll conducted by the *Harvard Crimson,* 57% of student respondents opposed Summers' resignation, with only 19% supporting it. ["Poll: Students Say Summers Should Stay," *The Harvard Crimson,* February 20, 2006]. Nevertheless, on the very next day after publication of this favourable poll, Summers announced his intention to resign as President of Harvard at the end of the school year. It is thought that the accusations of "sexism" also cost Summers the position of President Obama's Treasury Secretary, a post that he had previously held under Bill Clinton. (He was however appointed by Obama to the lesser post of Director of the National Economic Council).

The attack on Larry Summers is just part of a general onslaught against freedom of speech and academic freedom in universities in Britain and America. In the words of Joanna Williams of the University of Kent: "Instead of an intellectual robustness to challenge and debate views, academics are teaching that words can inflict violence and oppression and should be censored." [*Academic Freedom in an Age of Conformity*, 2016].

This call for censorship has been enthusiastically taken up by students on both sides of the Atlantic. At the time of writing there is a campaign among Oxford students to remove from Oriel College the prominent statue of the British mining magnate and imperialist politician, Cecil John Rhodes (1853-1902) – who provided the funds in his will for the famous Rhodes Scholarships, which have benefited generations of Commonwealth and American students. Similarly, in America there have been student demands for the removal from the campus of Princeton University of the name of President Woodrow Wilson, who had been president of the university before becoming US President, a position which he held from 1913 to 1921. Wilson's sin? While known internationally as a great liberal and founder of the League of Nations, in US domestic politics Wilson was responsible for reintroducing racial segregation in federal institutions in Washington DC.

Student opposition to free speech goes well beyond trying to obliterate unwelcome images of the past. In November 2014, a group of Oxford students managed to close down a debate organized by Oxford Students for Life, an anti-abortion group. One student calling for the cancellation of the debate remarked: "The idea that in a free society absolutely everything should be open to debate has a detrimental effect on marginalized groups." [Quoted by Joanna Williams, location 371]. In other words, the right not to be offended takes priority over freedom of speech.

A "culture of conformity" is increasingly dominant in academia. Hoff Somers comments: "Students are quick to learn that open criticism of the feminist classroom will not win them support from teachers who privately agree with them. The lesson they learn from the cravenness of their teachers is never lost on them: keep clear of controversy. Conformity is safest: practice it." [1994, p. 117].

In 2014 a Harvard student, Sandra Korn, writing in the student newspaper, exhorted her fellow students: "Let's give up on academic freedom in favor of justice." [Quoted Joanna Williams, location 2943]. Earlier similar formulations include this remark by Judith Butler: "Academic freedom is sometimes in conflict with basic human rights", and "when such conflicts occur it must be that basic human rights are the more important good to defend." [2006b].

Academic freedom is essentially a subset of freedom of speech. But is freedom of speech not itself a human right – a fundamental human right second to none? The guardians of what passes for "liberal democracy" certainly pay lip-service to freedom of speech as a supreme right. Freedom of speech is enshrined in the First Amendment to the US Constitution and is also placed high up in the British and European democratic pantheon, albeit with certain qualifications.

How could there possibly be any conflict between academic freedom and "basic human rights"? And what "basic human rights" are we talking about? The chief "human right" invoked by those who wish to curtail academic freedom -- and freedom of speech in general -- is the right not to be offended. But is there really such a right? Or, more to the point, should there be such a right? Even if it is agreed that there should be such a right, who is entitled to this right and who decides who is entitled to it?

"Je suis Charlie"

This whole issue came to a head in the wake of the murderous assault on the French satirical magazine, *Charlie Hebdo*, in January 2015, in which eight cartoonists and journalists, two police officers and two others were brutally killed by Islamist gunmen who objected to the magazine's critical cartoons of the prophet Muhammad. This attack aroused a sense of outrage throughout the Western world, with thousands of people sporting the slogan "Je suis Charlie". But sympathy for the victims was often tempered with criticism. Pope Francis remarked that, though freedom of expression is a "fundamental" human right, there are limits to that right. If someone "says a curse word against my mother, he can expect a punch. It's normal. It's normal. You cannot provoke. You cannot insult the faith of others. You cannot make fun of the faith of others....One cannot offend, make war, kill in the name of one's own religion–that is, in the name of God." [*Washington Post*, 15 January 2015].

This less than full-throated defence of free speech aroused a firestorm of criticism against the Pope. But how genuine were his critics themselves in their protestations of support for freedom of speech? Bernard Holtrop, a 73-year-old surviving Charlie Hebdo cartoonist, was certainly in no doubt. When asked what he thought of the apparent outpouring of sympathy from the European and international establishment, he replied: "We vomit on all these people who suddenly say they are our friends." [*New York Daily News*, 11 January 2015]. Immediately after the massacre, British Prime Minister David Cameron and Labour Party leader Ed Miliband stood shoulder to shoulder pledging to resist all attacks "on our democratic way of life and freedom of speech". In later interviews Cameron even added that "in a free society there is a right to cause offence about someone's religion" and: "We have to accept that newspapers, magazines, can publish things that are offensive to some, as long as it's within the law."

Trying to stop Charlie Hebdo from criticizing Islam is presumably contrary to "our democratic way of life and freedom of speech". But it's all right for the British Government itself to try to stop. Yet in 2014 no fewer than 1,209 people were found guilty in Britain of offences under section 127(1) of the Communications Act 2003 – up from just 143 in 2004. Their crime? Sending a telephone or social media message or email that is "grossly offensive or of an indecent, obscene or menacing character." [*Daily Telegraph*, 24 May 2015]. For a conviction under this section a message does not have to be threatening, only "grossly offensive". So much for David Cameron's remark about "the right to cause offence".

"Synthetic babies"
When Dolce and Gabbana, well-known gay Italian fashion designers, expressed the view that gay adoption of "synthetic" babies was "unnatural", they found themselves the objects of a "celebrity" social media boycott spearheaded by popular singer Sir Elton John. If one disagreed with Dolce and Gabbana, was it not enough simply to express one's disagreement without trying to destroy the designers' business?

Trumping President Trump
Blocking anyone whose views one finds offensive has now become a standard reaction not only among students and radical extremists but also more generally. So, when in 2017 President Trump of the US was invited by Theresa May to come to the UK on a state visit, the Speaker of the House of

Commons, John Bercow, himself lost no time in expressing his strong opposition to the President's addressing Parliament in Westminster Hall because of his allegedly "racist and sexist" views. John Bercow would no doubt consider himself a staunch believer in tolerance and freedom of speech – yet both those principles would be betrayed by his proposed action. At the time of writing President Trump's state visit has yet to take place, so it remains to be seen whether wiser counsels and more tolerant spirits will prevail over the Speaker's small-minded PC attitude.

"Prevent"

In June 2011, soon after Theresa May became British Home Secretary, she presented to Parliament a 111-page document with a bilious green cover titled *"Prevent Strategy"*, which set out an extension of the anti-radicalization policy initiated by the previous Labour government. "We remain absolutely committed to protecting freedom of speech in this country," crowed the bilious green booklet. "But preventing terrorism will mean challenging extremist (and non-violent) ideas that are also part of a terrorist ideology." [page 23]. This admission that non-violent ideas are to be targeted raises more questions than it answers. First of all, what is meant by non-violent extremist ideas "that are also part of a terrorist ideology"? Who is to decide what ideas fall into this category? How can such non-violent ideas be suppressed without curtailing freedom of speech? And, above all, how can a government programme that stigmatizes certain ideas and ways of thinking possibly succeed? Young people who are most susceptible to "non-violent extremist ideas" are already likely to be disaffected with the British Government and its vaunted "democratic way of life" and will not be slow to recognize that, far from protecting freedom of speech, the government's "Prevent" programme is actually an attempt to brainwash them – which will only serve to promote "extremism" rather than to combat it. Among other things, the programme obliges teachers to report to the police students whom they suspect of "radical behaviour". About 90% of such referrals have resulted in no further action being taken. But the Government has only redoubled its efforts. In her speech at the state opening of Parliament on 18 May 2016 the Queen announced: "Legislation will be introduced to prevent radicalization, tackle extremism in all its forms, and promote community integration." The Terrorism Act 2006 already criminalizes hate speech and the promotion of terrorism, but the proposed Counter-Extremism and Safeguarding Bill threatens to take this even further.

In Britain "offensive" but non-criminal behaviour of a sexual nature has recently come under the spotlight. John O'Neill, a 44-year-old Yorkshire man who had been acquitted of rape suddenly found himself the subject of a Sexual Risk Order requiring him to give the police the name, address and date of birth of any possible sexual partner "at least 24 hours prior to any sexual activity taking place" – "sexual activity" being defined to include kissing and even sexual conversation. Though acquitted of rape by a unanimous jury,

John O'Neill was gratuitously described by the trial judge as a "very dangerous man". His problem appears to have been that he gave the impression of having an interest in fetishism, which of course is not a crime. In fact, he had no criminal record, "not even a parking ticket". [*Daily Mail*, 14 July 2016].

"Support Gay Marriage"
The "gay cake" saga -- or at least the early stages of it -- was referred to in Chapter 1, but, though its subject matter may appear trivial, it actually engages several important legal principles and at the time of writing is on its way to the UK Supreme Court and possibly also the Strasbourg Human Rights court. In brief, a gay would-be customer placed an order with a bakery owned by a Christian couple to produce a cake proclaiming "Support Gay Marriage". The bakery owners turned the order down on religious grounds, but they were found by the Northern Ireland Court of Appeal to have discriminated against the gay prospective customer. [*Lee v. McArthur* [2016] NICA 29]. The bakery owners claimed that this was a case of "forced speech" and relied on their right to freedom of expression under ECHR Article 10. However, according to the Court of Appeal judgment: "It was not suggested [by the bakery owners] that there was any approbation of the message on the face of the cake and the trial judge concluded that what the respondent [prospective customer] wanted did not require them to promote or support gay marriage." The court added: "There is no challenge to that conclusion directly in the questions before

us and in any event we consider that the conclusion was undoubtedly correct. The fact that a baker provides a cake for a particular team or portrays witches on a Halloween cake does not indicate support for either." The logic of this argument leaves much to be desired. First, the fact that the bakery owners claimed that the "Support Gay Marriage" decoration on the proposed cake amounted to "forced speech" is surely indicative in itself of the fact that baking that cake would or at least could have been taken as constituting support for gay marriage. Secondly, the analogy with sport or Halloween is a false analogy, bringing the whole argument crashing down to the ground. Unlike the examples given, "Support Gay Marriage" is a political slogan actually inviting support in a very direct way. The outcome of the case can only mean that gay rights -- including gay people's right of freedom of expression -- trump the bakery owners' right to freedom of expression, not to mention their right to freedom of religion under ECHR Article 9 and their ordinary common law rights as tradespeople to accept or reject any contract proposed to them. It remains to be seen how this case fares in the UK Supreme Court and possibly the European Court of Human Rights. However, if recent trends are anything to go by, "political correctness" in the shape of gay rights will probably triumph again. But the point is that it is not just gay *rights* that have triumphed so far: it is *special privileges* for gays.

Students at Oxford University have been asked by a students' union leaflet to use "gender neutral" pronouns

instead of "he" or "she" when referring to other people. The pronoun of choice is "ze", which is also promoted for use by university teachers in lectures and tutorials.
[www.newsmax.com – 12 December 2016].

There is already an array of gender-neutral pronouns in use at various American universities. These include (in addition to "ze), "xe"'"zer" "hir", "e", "ey" and "per"! The University of Michigan recently informed all students and faculty of the introduction of "a process for students to designate pronouns with the University and have those pronouns reflected on class rosters this fall". A student named Grant Strobl had the last laugh at this policy by announcing: "I henceforth shall be referred to as: His Majesty Grant Strobl." [www.thecollegefix.com – 28 September 2016].

It is easy to dismiss this whole issue as a joke, except that it appears to be gaining ground, especially at universities, and, as usual with "political correctness", far from representing tolerance and openness, it marks yet a further milestone towards irrationality and control. A professor at the University of Toronto, Canada, who has fallen foul of the "speech police", has had his office door lock glued shut, has been reprimanded by university authorities and could even conceivably be fired from his job. Professor Jordan Peterson has had the courage or the foolhardiness to announce that he (yes, he) will not use "gender neutral" pronouns even when referring to someone who has expressed a preference to be described in that way. [www.bbc.co.uk – 4 November 2016]. Nicholas Matte, another faculty member at the same university, strenuously opposes Peterson: "Basically, it's not correct that there is such a thing as biological sex." [*www.thecollegefix.com*–1 December 2016].

This makes no sense at all. There undoubtedly are major differences between male and female – anatomical, physiological and psychological. The word "gender" now tends to be used in a different sense from "sex". According to the *Oxford English Dictionary* ,"sex" tends now to refer to biological differences", while "gender" "often intends to emphasize the social and cultural, as opposed to the biological, distinctions between the sexes." A small minority of human beings, who are born with ambiguous genitalia, are now termed "intersex". Until the mid-twentieth century the term "hermaphrodite" (a combination of the names of the Greek gods Hermes and Aphrodite) was used interchangeably with "intersex", but it has now largely gone out of use, partly at least because it was regarded as derogatory.

A much more prominent and vocal element in UK society today is made up of the "transgender" – or simply "trans" – community. According to a report by the House of Commons Women and Equalities Committee, there are as many as 650,000 people in the UK who are "gender incongruent to some degree". [BBC.co.uk – 14 January 2016]. The older term "transsexual" is now used to describe "the subset of transgender people who desire to transition permanently to the gender with which they identify and who seek medical assistance (for example, sex reassignment surgery) with this". [Wikipedia, "Transgender"].

Both "transgender" and "transsexual" must of course be differentiated from "tranvestite", which refers simply to (usually only occasional) cross-dressing without any necessary desire to "transition" one's birth sex or gender identification.

Transgender
The most fashionable aspect of "political correctness" now is that associated with "transgender". "Misgendering" a trans person can land you in court, as happened to Vernon Mussington when he greeted a male-to-female transgender person "all right geezer". Mr Mussington claimed that he did not realize that the person he was addressing was transgender, but, on the basis of having greeted the same person in this fashion on three separate occasions, he was convicted of harassment by magistrates and sentenced to 150 hours' community service and a fine of £360. On appeal to the Crown Court he was acquitted, but only because the prosecution was able to prove only one of the three alleged incidents, yet the judge still condemned Vernon Mussington's conduct as "offensive and abusive" to the complainant, who had been allowed to testify from behind a screen. It is hard to disagree with Mr Mussington's comment after his acquittal: "I've been under constant stress for nearly a year because of this. I can't believe anyone could end up in court for saying 'all right geezer'. It's absurd." [*Daily Mail* 3 February 2017]. It's also disquieting that freedom of speech is now so precarious. This is no isolated incident. The complainant in Vernon

Mussington's case was 47 years old, began "transitioning" in 2014 and claimed to be shortly about to have surgery. Yet even children who have decided that they are "a female trapped in a male body", or vice versa, are now allowed to demand to be treated as belonging to their chosen gender.

The Boy Scouts of America recently lifted the ban on gay adults as scout leaders only two years after allowing openly gay boys to join scouting. Now, in 2017, the Boy Scouts of America have announced that their policy now permits transgender boys to join–gender being whatever the prospective member chooses to write on their application form. This change of policy comes hard on the heels of an announcement that an 8-year-old "trans boy" is suing the New Jersey Boy Scouts' Council after he was kicked out of the troop for his gender identity. The British Scout Association similarly announces on its website that it is "open to all young people regardless of their gender identity". [members.scouts.org.uk].

At first sight, there would appear to be a contradiction between the fashionable clamour for gender-neutral pronouns and the equally fashionable demand for transgender rights. Most transgender people want to be recognized in their chosen gender and therefore want all the rights associated with that – including name-change and the use of bathrooms intended for people of that birth-gender. This is not the same as wanting gender-neutral pronouns or facilities, which is logically explicable as a desire not to want to be defined in terms of one's sex or gender.

What the two groups have in common is a demand for special privileges couched in the language of equality. This demand has already been met to some extent. The Gender Recognition Act 2004 was passed in response to Strasbourg court rulings, notably the case of *Christine Goodwin v. UK* [2002] 2 FCR 577. Christine Goodwin was a post-operative male-to-female transsexual who claimed to have suffered sexual harassment at work and also objected to the fact that her unchanged National Insurance number enabled her employer to discover her previous identity. She won in Strasbourg under ECHR Article 8 (right to respect for private life and family life) and Article 12 (right to marry and found a family) and was awarded a payment of EUR 239,000.

Gender Recognition Act 2004

The Gender Recognition Act 2004 gives people with "gender dysphoria" legal recognition as members of their acquired gender, including the right to obtain a new birth certificate and marrying. There are several alternative ways of applying for these special privileges granted by a "gender recognition certificate" issued by a Gender Recognition Panel, but the main route entails an application to a Gender Recognition Panel, which must grant the application if it is "satisfied" that the applicant (a) "has or has had gender dysphoria", (b) has lived in the acquired gender for at least two years, and (c) produces a relevant report from a medical practitioner or psychologist.

"Gender dysphoria" or "gender identity disorder" is "the dysphoria (distress) a person experiences as a result of the sex and gender they were assigned at birth. In these cases, the assigned sex and gender do not match the person's gender identity, and the person is transgender", [Wikipedia, "Gender dysphoria"].

This remarkable legislation therefore makes the UK government complicit in falsifying a person's sex at birth with a view to misleading prospective employers and even prospective marriage partners! What is more, although a medical evidence of "gender dysphoria" is required, the applicant does not need to have undergone any "gender reassignment" surgery nor have any desire to do so in the future. This means that someone with male genitalia can legally be treated as female and even marry another male provided s/he has lived as a female for two years and is suffering from the very vaguely defined "gender dysphoria".

Transgender Problems

Besides the issues surrounding the issues of rights and special privileges, there are much more serious questions about the medical and psychological aspects of "transitioning" from one sex or gender to the other. "According to studies in America and Holland, around one in 20 post-operative transsexuals changes his or her mind after surgery, and around one in ten never adjusts and often becomes deeply depressed." [Sarah Lonsdale, "When sex-change is a mistake" -- Independent.co.uk – 23 October 1993]. In some cases people have "transitioned" more than once. The case of Mark/Marissa Dainton/Patricia Vincent is an example, who "changed sex" three times in 11 years. [David Batty, "Mistaken identity", *The Guardian*, 31 July 2004]. Birmingham University's Aggressive Research Intelligence Facility (ARIF), which reviews healthcare treatments for the NHS, asked to assess the findings of more than 100 follow-up studies of post-operative transsexuals, reported that "none of the studies provides conclusive evidence that gender reassignment is beneficial for patients. It found that most research was poorly designed, which skewed the results in favour of physically changing sex. There was no evaluation of whether other treatments, such as long-term counselling, might help transsexuals, or whether their gender confusion might lessen over time." [Ibid]. "Dr Chris Hyde, director of ARIF, is quoted as saying: There is huge uncertainty over whether changing someone's sex is a good or a bad thing. While no doubt great care is taken to ensure that appropriate patients undergo gender reassignment, there's still a large number of people who have the surgery but remain traumatised – often to the point of committing suicide."

Some of the complaints against Russell Reid were brought by four other doctors who specialise in treating gender identity disorders. Dr Kevan Wylie, a psychiatrist: "There is currently no consensus on treatment."

Alan Finch, an Australian who underwent male-female "gender reassignment" surgery at the age of 21, soon came to regret the change and lashed out at what he called the "sex change industry" and argued that "transsexualism was invented by psychiatrists". "Their language is illusory. You fundamentally can't change sex. The surgery doesn't alter you genetically. It's genital mutilation. My 'vagina' was just the bag of my scrotum. It's like a pouch, like a kangaroo. What's scary is you still feel like you have a penis when you're sexually aroused. It's like a phantom limb syndrome. It's all been a terrible misadventure. I've never been a woman, just Alan."[Ibid]. Few victims of the "sex change industry" have the insight or the courage to speak out in this way. And those who do, including Alan Finch himself, have been effectively silenced by "trans" activists. ["Trouble in Transtopia: Murmurs of Sex Change Regret ", *The Federalist*, 11 November 2014]. Perhaps it is time to bring back into use those completely politically incorrect words, *eunuch* and *castration*, to refer to the victims of the "sex change industry".

****

CHAPTER 6
Do You Have a Right of Privacy?

Principles

ECHR Article 8 declares:

"1. Everyone has the right to respect for his private and family life, his home and his correspondence.

2. There shall be no interference by a public authority with the exercise of this right except such as is in accordance with the law and is necessary in a democratic society in the interests of national security, public safety or the economic well-being of the country, for the prevention of disorder or crime, for the protection of health or morals, or for the protection of the rights and freedoms of others."

There are three important points to note in connection with this Article:

a) It does not confer a right of *privacy*. The word "privacy" does not even appear, only the term "private and family life".

b) In common with the rest of the ECHR, it has *vertical* effect only, not horizontal. In other words, it is about protection from "public authorities", not from another person or private entity.

c) It is in direct competition with ECHR Article 6, Freedom of Expression, and section 12 of the HRA, which elevates freedom of expression -- and, in particular, freedom of the press -- above all other Convention rights.

Kaye v. Robertson (1991)

The English common law has never contained any protection of privacy. This was highlighted by the case of *Kaye v. Robertson* [1991] FSR 62. Gorden Kaye, a popular television actor, was badly injured in a freak accident when a piece of wood smashed his car windscreen and hit him on the head. After a 5½ hour brain operation and three days in intensive care he was moved to a private ward. Ignoring notices in the corridor and on the ward door itself, a newspaper reporter and photographer from the *Sunday Sport* entered the actor's room. Gorden Kaye apparently agreed to talk to them and did not object to their photographing his head swathed in bandages. However, according to medical evidence, the actor was in no fit state to give informed consent. At first instance Gorden Kaye was granted an injunction against the newspaper, but this was reversed on appeal. Lord Justice Bingham was prepared to stigmatize the newspaper's action as "a monstrous invasion of his privacy". But he regretted that an invasion of privacy alone, however gross, did not give rise to a cause of action under the existing law. Lord Justice Glidewell gave voice to an eloquent plea to Parliament: "It is well known that in English law there is no right to privacy, and accordingly there is no right for breach of a person's privacy. The facts of the present case are a graphic illustration of the desirability of Parliament considering whether and in

What circumstances statutory provision can be made to protect the privacy of individuals."

However galling this result may have been to Gorden Kaye, it was the right decision and it respected the proper limits of judicial power. It was not for the courts to make law. That was the function of Parliament. However, needless to say, Lord Justice Glidewell's heartfelt yet perfectly proper plea to Parliament fell on deaf ears. In keeping with a long tradition of lethargy and dereliction of duty on the part of Parliament -- and the Government -- nothing was done. It was into this vacuum that the courts were to move by expanding the common law cause of action of breach of confidence and also the scope of ECHR Article 8. Judicial activist law-making, however well-intentioned, is not only wrong but generally causes more problems than it solves.

Mr Justice Eady, the leading libel judge between 1997 and 2013, was later to remark that there was "a serious gap in the jurisprudence of any civilized society, if such a gross intrusion could happen without redress." ["Decisions of the 'privacy law judge', *news.bbc.co.uk*–10 November 2008]. David Eady was a member of the Calcutt committee set up in 1989 to consider, among other things, the introduction of a privacy law. Eady favoured this, but it was opposed by powerful interests in the media, so nothing happened. Not even the Calcutt report's recommendation to make intrusion a criminal offence was acted upon. Calcutt's proposed Press Complaints Commission, which was actually set up, turned into a damp squib, to be replaced in 2014 by an equally ineffectual voluntary "press regulator" known as the Independent Press Standards Organisation (Ipso), which was soon denounced as a "sham body controlled by the newspapers" that it is meant to regulate. [See Jasper Jackson, *The Guardian*, 8 September 2015].

The English judge Lord Hoffmann poured scorn on Judge Bostjan Zupancic, a Slovenian judge sitting on the Strasbourg court, for remarking that "the courts have to some extent and under American influence made a fetish of the freedom of the press". [Hoffmann, "The Universality of Human Rights", Judicial Studies Board Annual Lecture, 2009]. In fact, the courts to which the distinguished Slovenian judge was referring were the German courts, but his remark was also to some extent -- and with some notable exceptions, like Eady J. -- applicable to Britain, where journalists are practically the only profession not subject to proper independent regulation and where press freedom -- as distinct from general freedom of speech -- is specially protected by law, in section 12 of the Human Rights Act 1998.

The balance between privacy and press freedom was redressed to some extent by Eady J., who was often accused of creating a right of privacy by the back door. But judge-made law is not the answer. Parliament should have responded to Lord Justice Glidewell's plea for legislation in the wake of the Gorden Kaye case in 1991. Judge Zupancic's suggested test in this area, based on the case of *Halford v. United Kingdom* ([1997] ECHR 32), is not to be sneezed at: the test of a "reasonable expectation of privacy". But this needs to be enshrined in legislation to avoid becoming messy.

Douglas v. Hello! (2001)

Eady J was not the only judge who tried to tried to step into the breach created by the Government and Parliament's dereliction of duty in this regard. The high-profile case of *Douglas v. Hello!* [2001] 2 All ER 289 is a good example. When Michael Douglas and Catherine Zeta-Jones tied the knot at the Plaza Hotel in New York in November 2000 they had already sold the exclusive rights to photograph their wedding to *OK!* Magazine for a fee of £1 million. Elaborate precautions were taken to protect *OK!*'s exclusive deal, including a ban on all cameras and recording devices at the reception. Despite this, *OK!*'s bitter rivals, *Hello!* magazine managed to get hold of pictures of the reception. Douglas and Zeta-Jones went to court to stop publication of these "unauthorized" pictures. Lord Justice Sedley in the Court of Appeal went so far as to suggest that "we have reached a point at which it can be said with confidence that the law recognizes and will appropriately protect a right of personal privacy." Sedley LJ also expressed the view that ECHR Article 8 -- and, balancing it, section 12 of the HRA -- had horizontal effect. The view that Article 8 now encompassed protection of privacy was not yet shared in the judiciary. Mr Justice Lindsay, the judge in the substantive trial, expressly declined what he called the invitation to hold "that there is an existing law of privacy" under which Michael Douglas, Catherine Zeta-Jones and OK!

Magazine were entitled to relief. But, while failing in their claim based on privacy, they succeeded under the law of confidence or confidentiality. [2003] EWHC 786.

This decision was reversed by the Court of Appeal and then reversed back again – yo-yo like – by a 3:2 majority in the House of Lords. [*OBG v. Allan* [2007] UKHL 21] The majority agreed with Lindsay J and restored his finding of a breach of confidence by *Hello!*. Lord Hoffmann put it this way: The photographer who took the "unauthorized" pictures was subject to an obligation of confidence in respect of the pictures which he took. *Hello!*...were subject to the same obligation." Really?

How could the freelance photographer or *Hello!* have been bound by a confidentiality agreement to which they were not parties?

The leading case of the common law of breach of confidence is *Coco v. A.N. Clark (Engineers) Ltd* [1969] RPC 41, in which Megarry J., one of the most distinguished judges of the twentieth century, identified the three essential ingredients of this cause of action:

a) "The information itself must have the necessary quality of confidence about it.

b) Secondly, that information must have been imparted in circumstances importing an obligation of confidence.

c) Thirdly, there must be an unauthorized use of that information to the detriment of the party communicating it."

So, there has to be an existing relationship between the parties prior to any such alleged breach. In the *Coco* case the plaintiff designed a two-stroke engine for a moped and sought the co-operation of the defendant company in its manufacture. However, after Coco had disclosed all the details of his design and proposals for its manufacture, the parties fell out and the defendants manufactured their own engine based on a design closely resembling Coco's. The defendants denied that any confidential information had been supplied to them by Coco or used by them in their engine. In *Coco v. Clark* itself no breach of confidence was found. Of the three essential ingredients only the second was held to exist. In *Douglas v. Hello!* it would be hard to find any of the three elements. There was no relationship or indeed contact of any kind between the parties; no confidential information was imparted by the Claimants to the Defendant, *Hello!* magazine; and *Hello!* made no use of any information obtained from either Douglas and Zeta-Jones or from *OK!* Did *Hello!* know that the Douglases had given an exclusive contract to their arch-rival magazine? Undoubtedly, but this was not information used by *Hello!* to compete with OK! Magazine. *Hello!* magazine used different photographs from the ones taken by OK! All that *Hello!* could really be said to have done wrong was to have trespassed on a wedding reception to which neither they nor the freelance photographer from whom they had bought their pictures had been invited. Trying to classify this case as one of breach of confidence is simply a stretch too far and amounts to judge-made law.

The two dissenting judges in the House of Lords were on stronger ground. Lord Nicholls flatly rejected OK!'s claim of confidentiality: "OK's claim is that Hello committed a breach of confidence by publishing a confidential secret...So the first step is to identify the 'secret'. The secret information cannot lie in the differences between the unapproved photographs and the approved photographs. The secret cannot lie there, because the six unapproved photographs contained nothing not included in the approved photographs...The expression of the bride in one wedding photograph compared with her expression in another is insufficiently significant to call for legal protection...Accordingly, once the approved pictures were published, albeit simultaneously, publication of the unapproved pictures was not a breach of confidence...For these reasons I am unable to accept OK's claim based on confidentiality." Lord Walker, agreeing with Lord Nicholls, summed up his logical position in these words: "My Lords, my respectful dissent from the views of the majority arises not from any distaste for the modern celebrity world but from my perception (shared, no doubt, by all of us) of the need for consistent and rational development in the law of confidentiality." [*OBG v. Allan* [2007] UKHL 21].

Mosley v. News Group Newspapers (2008)
The judge-made law of breach of confidence reached its apogee in *Mosley v. News Group Newspapers* [2008] EWHC 1777 (QB), the *News of the World*, a mass-circulation Sunday newspaper, published a front-page story headed "F1 Boss has

Sick Nazi Orgy with 5 Hookers". The article concerned Max Mosley, president of the Fédération Internationale de l'Automobile and son of Sir Oswald Mosley, leader of the British Union of Fascists during the 1930s. It had a subheading reading: "Son of Hitler-loving fascist in sex shame." The claim was not for defamation but for "breach of confidence and/or the unauthorized disclosure of personal information" infringing Max Mosley's rights under EVHR Article 8. Max Mosley won the case and was awarded £60,000 in damages, which he claimed was far less than his legal costs.

It is important to note that Article 8 does not protect *privacy* as such, and the word "privacy" does not appear in Article 8, only the term "private life". Max Mosley's legal representatives sought to bridge this gap by arguing, as explained by the judge, "not only that the content of the published material was inherently private in nature, consisting as it did of the portrayal of sado-masochistic ('S and M') and some sexual activities, but that there had also been a pre-existing relationship of confidentiality between the participants. They had all known each other for some time and took part in such activities on the understanding that they would be private and that none of them would reveal what had taken place. I was told that there is a fairly tight-knit community of S and M activists on what is known as 'the scene' and that it is an unwritten rule that people are trusted not to reveal what has gone on. That is hardly surprising."

As the claim was against a newspaper group, not against other participants in the party, it is hard to see what relevance this "confidentiality" could possibly have. There certainly was no relationship of confidence or confidentiality between Max Mosley and the Publishers of the *News of the World*.

But the judge, David Eady J., did not base his decision on the relationship of confidentiality that was alleged to exist between the participants in the party. Instead, he relied on a line of recent cases which had extended the law of "old-fashioned breach of confidence": "The law now affords protection to information in respect of which there is a reasonable expectation of privacy, even in circumstances where there is no pre-existing relationship giving rise of itself to an enforceable duty of confidence." Rejecting the allegations of a Nazi theme to the party and finding that there was no "public interest justification" for publication of the story, the judge concluded that Max Mosley "had a reasonable expectation of privacy in relation to sexual activities (albeit unconventional) carried on between consenting adults on private property".

After winning his case in the English High Court, Max Mosley filed an application to the European Court of Human Rights in Strasbourg claiming that his Article 8 rights "were violated by the UK's failure to impose a legal duty on the *News of the World* to notify him in advance in order to allow him the opportunity to seek an interim injunction and thus prevent publication of material which violated his right to respect for his private life". The Strasbourg court rejected Max Mosley's application, on the grounds of (a) "the limited scope under Article 10 for restriction on the freedom of the press to publish material which contributes to debate on matters of general public interest"; (b) "the chilling effect to which a pre-notification requirement risks giving rise", (c) "the significant doubts as to the effectiveness of any pre-notification requirement"; and (d) the wide margin of appreciation in this area". The Strasbourg court therefore was "of the view that Article 8 does not require a legally binding pre-notification requirement".

Accordingly, the Court concludes that there has been no violation of Article 8 of the Convention by the absence of such a requirement in domestic law." [*Mosley v. UK* [2011] 53 EHRR 30].

This case is only one of a number of English cases in which a hugely expanded "breach of confidence" meets a greatly extended ECHR Article 8. This has largely been the work of the UK domestic courts and what it is really doing is filling the vacuum of a true law of privacy, which exists neither at common law nor in ECHR Article 8.

It was this dereliction of duty on the part of the Government and Parliament -- possibly prompted by a fear of the press -- that created a vacuum into which the courts stepped with their "backdoor" law of privacy. Besides amounting to judicial usurpation of the legislative function of Parliament, this judge-made law, as is practically inevitable with any judge-made law, is unclear or even muddled.

In particular, what *are* the criteria for deciding whether a publication should be protected as being "in the public interest" or whether it breaches some actionable right which is entitled to legal protection?

There are no clear criteria, and it is not always even possible to test the courts' reasoning, because of the rise of the "super-injunction", defined in 2011 by the Neuberger Committee, set up to examine the law and practice of super-injunctions, as: "an interim injunction which restrains a person from (i) publishing information which concerns the applicant and is said to be confidential or private; and (ii) publicizing or informing others of the existence of the order and the proceedings (the 'super' element of the order)." Because of their secrecy, it is not even known how many super-injunctions have been issued, and, in keeping with Government supineness, no government department has kept track or these injunctions and no record is kept of them.

In May 2011 the *Daily Telegraph* estimated that that 80 "gagging orders" had been issued in the previous six years. The beneficiaries of these orders included: "nine footballers, nine actors, four pop stars, six wealthy businessmen and women, a senior civil servant and an MP."
[www.telegraph.co.uk – 18 May 2011].

So, if you like the idea of a gagging order to stop the press revealing your indiscretions, think again – unless you happen to be a "celebrity" or a billionaire.

"The Snooper's Charter"

The Investigatory Powers Act 2016, dubbed by opponents the "snooper's charter", received the royal assent in November

2016 – after a five-year battle involving three independent reviews before a draft Bill was even published and then reviews by three parliamentary committees. It was described by David Cameron as "going "to the heart of the Government's duty to keep the British public safe". But the Act's requirement for all internet records to be stored for 12 months is characterized by opponents as a major extension of the Government's surveillance powers, though some security experts believe that the data overload will actually hamper the security services in their attempt to identify offenders. Jonathan Evans (now Lord Evans of Weardale), Director-General of MI5 from 2007 to 2013, comments: "From my time in MI5 I know that we had more than enough to do without wasting our time spying on ordinary members of the public. Even if we had thought that this was a good idea, the new controls mean that we would need the agreement not only of a government minister but also of a senior judge before we could proceed. Moreover, the new Act lays down clear sanctions for misuse of the powers." [*The Telegraph*, 9 December 2016].

The National Crime Agency (NCA), which is responsible for investigating organized crime, including human, weapon and drug trafficking, cyber crime, economic crime and terrorism, explained that the internet connection records (ICR) which it investigates will look like this:

| Date/Time | Mobile No. | Source IP | Source Port | Dest IP | Postcode | Domain |

This information, likened to an "itemized phone bill", will not identify any names, bank account numbers or even email addresses – and certainly not any of the content of the listed phone-calls. The information collected is what is referred to as *metadata*, meaning "information that provides information about other data".

The Act introduces a "double lock" for oversight. To obtain the content of a communication, the police will require an "intercept warrant", which will require ministerial authorization and then be put forward to a panel of judges, who will have the power to veto it. This panel will be overseen by a senior judge known as the "Investigatory Powers Commissioner".

It remains to be seen whether the many concessions to opponents made by the Government in the new law will finally allow the Government to do its job of protecting the safety and security of the nation. On 8 December 2016 Alex Younger, the head of MI6, the UK's secret intelligence service, warned of the severity of the terrorist threat to the UK: "The scale of the threat is unprecedented. The UK intelligence and security services have disrupted 12 terrorist plots since June 2013. And MI5 and the police continue to run hundreds of investigations into those intent on carrying out or supporting terrorist atrocities against our citizens." He added that the internet and data had turned the business of spying "on its head". "They represent an existential threat combined with a golden opportunity." [*Daily Mail*, 8 December 2016].

In January 2015 Sir John Sawers, the head of MI6 from 2009 to 2014, went so far as to warn that "a successful terrorist attack on the UK by Islamic militants is all but inevitable", adding that the UK security services will not be able to prevent terrorism unless they monitor the internet traffic of innocent people. "There is a dilemma because the general public, politicians and technology companies, to some extent, want us to be able to monitor the activities of terrorists and other evil-doers but they don't want their own activities to be open to any such monitoring....The benefit of the last 18 months' debate is that people now understand that is not possible, and there has to be some form of ability to cover communications that are made through modern technology....If you do not have any security then all your basic freedoms are at threat." He added, chillingly: "We are not saying that an attempted terror attack is highly likely, but that an attack actually getting through is highly likely....At some point a threat will get through." [David Barrett & Colin Freeman, *The Telegraph*, 20 January 2015].

The "politically correct" hysteria about privacy does not appear to be as widespread as we are often led to believe. A survey conducted by the Edelman Trust Barometer, an international survey of public trust in public institutions, indicated that the UK public had far more trust in the intelligence agencies than in other official bodies: 64% expressing trust in MI6 and 72% in MI5, as against 43% for government overall. [David Barrett & Colin Freeman, *The Telegraph*, 20 January 2015].

The Investigatory Powers Act 2016 is only the latest of several attempts by the UK Government to give the security services powers relating to telephonic and internet records.

The previous short-lived attempt was made by the Data Retention and Investigatory Powers Act (DRIPA) 2014, whose validity was challenged in court by two members of Parliament, one Conservative and the other Labour. The Divisional Court ruled in their favour, holding that section 1 of DRIPA was "inconsistent with European Union law".

This section allowed the Government to "require a public telecommunications operator to retain relevant communications data" for 12 months. DRIPA was passed with Liberal Democrat and Labour support in return for the introduction of a new "privacy and civil liberties board" to oversee the security services and act as an independent watchdog. But that did not satisfy the Divisional Court, because there was no provision for "prior review" by "a court or independent administrative board", which the Divisional Court held was required by EU law. (*R (David Davis & Tom Watson) v. Secretary of State* [2015] EWHC 2092 (Admin), §114).

The Court of Appeal doubted that there was any such provision in EU law and referred the case to the European Court of Justice. (*Secretary of State for Home Dept v. David Davis & Tom Watson* [2015] EWCA Civ 1185).

In the European Court of Justice (ECJ) itself, the conclusion of the Advocate General was generally favourable to the UK Government: "Articles 7, 8 and 52(1) of the Charter of Fundamental Rights of the European Union are to be interpreted as not precluding Member States from imposing on providers of electronic communications services an obligation to retain all data relating to communications effected by the users of their services," subject to certain conditions, notably that "the obligation must be strictly necessary in the fight against serious crime". [*Secretary of State for the Home Dept v. Tom Watson*, Opinion of Advocate General Saugmandsgaard Oe, 19 July 2016, Joined cases C-203/15 and C-698/15 curia.europa.eu].

The Grand Chamber of 15 judges of the ECJ, in a decision handed down on 21 December 2016, was less favourable to the UK Government, ruling that "general and indiscriminate retention" of emails and electronic communications by governments is illegal. [Owen Bowcott, Guardian, 21 December 2016]. "Only targeted interception of traffic and location data in order to combat serious crime–including terrorism–is justified." The case has now been remitted to the UK's Court of Appeal to be resolved in terms of UK legislation. The court pointed out that electronic communications allow "very precise conclusions to be drawn concerning the private lives of persons whose data has been retained......The interference by national legislation that provides for the retention of traffic data and location data with that right must therefore be considered to be particularly serious. The fact that the data is retained without the users of electronic communications services being informed of the fact is likely to cause the persons concerned to feel that their private lives are the subject of constant surveillance. Consequently, only the objective of fighting serious crime is capable of justifying such interference. Legislation prescribing a general and indiscriminate retention of data....exceeds the limits of what is strictly necessary and cannot be considered to be justified within a democratic society." Prior authorization by a court or independent body to access retained data is required for each official request, held the ECJ.

David Davis, who dropped out of the case after becoming Secretary of State for leaving the EU, had previously commented that the British Government were "treating the entire nation as suspects". A conclusive reply to this was given by Lord Hague, the former Foreign Secretary, in an eloquent and wide-ranging article:

"Winning the battle against mass murder on the streets will need this paranoia to be overcome...The interception of the contents of an individual's communications in this country can only be carried out with a warrant signed by a senior minister. For four years, I was one of those ministers, and if people could see–which they obviously can't–the time, care and detail spent on each case, including by the minister, I believe they would be greatly reassured. It is only after reading a clear justification and exhaustive legal advice that a minister signs that warrant, or doesn't. How he or she does that work is reviewed every year by an independent commissioner. And the new Bill before Parliament will mean a judge will review the warrants as well. Yet the cracking of terrorist and criminal networks requires not only such interception but also access to 'bulk data'. This logs which internet sites were visited on which device, and which device was used to contact another one. It is vital in order to see patterns in the behavior of those who might join a cell such as the one in Brussels. And it can help us to spot them if they make a mistake. Over the next few months, Parliament will engage in the centuries-old debate about how to balance privacy and security. It should recognise that collecting bulk data is not the same as mass surveillance, and learn a key lesson of Brussels: beating this terror will need every legitimate tool that a free society can employ." [*Telegraph*, 28 March 2016].

So, what about the Divisional Court's insistence on "prior review by a court or independent administrative board"? There is no such requirement in law. Both Sir Anthony May, the Interception of Communications Commissioner (ICC) and his predecessor Sir Paul Kennedy – both former Court of Appeal judges – "had consistently been of the view that the requirement for judicial approval would not be likely to lead to improved standards or 'have any impact other than to introduce unnecessary bureaucracy into the process and increase the costs associated with acquiring the data'". (*R (David Davis & Tom Watson) v. Secretary of State* [2015] EWHC 2092 (Admin), §78).

Another much more serious objection to the requirement of prior judicial approval is that this is quite likely to lead to the frustration of the whole system by "politically correct" judges, thus reducing the protection of the ordinary law-abiding majority from crime and terrorism.

The comment of then Home Office Security Minister, John Hayes, on the original Divisional Court decision is instructive: "We disagree absolutely with this judgment and will seek an appeal. Communications data is not just crucial in the investigation of serious crime. It is also a fundamental part of investigating other crimes which still have a severe impact, such as stalking and harassment, as well as locating missing people, including vulnerable people who have threatened to commit suicide." And again: "The effect of this judgment would be that in certain cases, communication data that could potentially save lives would only be available to the police and other law enforcement if a communications company had decided to retain it for commercial reasons. We believe that is wrong. I do think there is a risk here of giving succour to the paranoid liberal bourgeoisie whose peculiar fears are placed ahead of the interests of the people." [Owen Bowcott, *The Guardian*, 17 July 2015].

John Hayes put his finger on the central issue here. Security laws do not threaten the human rights of the law-abiding majority, they protect those rights. Kowtowing to the "peculiar fears" of the "paranoid liberal bourgeoisie", in his graphic phrase, is at the expense of the interests of the people as a whole. Why does the "politically correct" "civil liberties" lobby not realize this? As Sir John Sawers of the MI6 pointed out (see above): "If you do not have any security then all your basic freedoms are under threat."

Interestingly enough, there is broad support in UK public opinion for increased surveillance powers on the part of the security services. According to Yougov on 18 January 2015, a majority of 53% of those surveyed (as against 31%) agreed that "phone and internet companies should be required to retain everyone's internet browsing history, emails, voice calls, social media interactions and mobile messaging, which the police and intelligence agencies would be able to access for anti-terrorism purposes."

Scrapping of ID Card Scheme

In the meantime the British Government, in a fit of mindless libertarian zeal, had started dismantling some important security protections – under the mistaken impression that this was in the interests of individual liberty. On 10 February 2011, Immigration Minister Damian Green gleefully fed into a giant shredder the last batch of 500 hard drives containing what was to be the national identity register, remarking: "this marks the final end of the identity card scheme: dead, buried and crushed." Although scrapping the scheme would save money, that, said Green, was not the reason for its cancellation. "We wanted to do this as a matter of principle." What principle could that possibly be? The Liberal Democrat Deputy Prime Minister was quick to explain: "The ID card scheme was a direct assault on our liberty, something too precious to be tossed aside, and something which this government is determined to restore. The government is committed to rolling back as much state interference as humanly possible, and the destruction of the register is only the beginning." [*samathieson.com*–10 February 2011]. However, there was still an ID card scheme in place for non-EU citizens involving the collection of biometric data. Damian Green justified this by claiming "that residency permits have a benefit to the holder, that of allowing them to seek employment". So, do ID cards for citizens not confer any benefits on their holders? "The ID card," opined the delirious minister, "represented the worst of government. The first duty of government is to ensure its citizens are protected, but ID cards could never have done that. They would have been a distraction from the real work that needs to be done in countering terrorism, illegal immigration or benefit fraud." [*The Guardian*, 21 December 2010]. Fortunately, the UK's security services have managed to foil a number of terrorist outrages, but illegal immigration and benefit fraud have escalated out of control. Is it a surprise that it is harder to control immigration and benefit fraud blindfold than with proper databases? On illegal immigration, the position according to Migration Watch UK is that: "Accurate numbers are not possible but there could be as many as one million illegal immigrants in the UK." And: "Removals of immigration offenders are very low. A significant increase in resources for this purpose is essential."

There are very few Western countries that do not have some form of national identity card, which is usually compulsory. In the USA, the land of the automobile, a driver's licence is usually required for ID purposes – very often together with a second form of ID. Non-drivers can go to their local Department of Motor Vehicles, where on payment of a small fee they will be issued with a card which to all intents and purposes is a driving licence, except for the wording around the edge: "This is not a driver's licence".

CCTV Under Attack
CCTV cameras are also being dismantled in a fit of false economy around the UK, with Westminster Council in the vanguard, which in 2016 axed its entire CCTV network of 75 cameras. But terror and policing expert David Videcette has commented: "All council CCTV networks are a massive resource to police, have a massive impact on bringing down anti-social behaviour, crime, drug dealing, they are very, very valuable to police....It's crazy–the money the council will spend on putting things right, vandalism, theft from local authority premises, it will pay for itself twice over. And there's a risk if there was a terrorist attack and we had to track a terrorist's movements." "Statistics provided by Westminster Council itself show that its network of CCTV cameras records about 600 criminal incidents a month leading to around 1,300 arrests a year. However, the dismantling of Westminster Council's CCTV network will not leave the city bereft of CCTV coverage, as the numerous CCTV cameras belonging to Transport for London and private companies are not affected. [*www.bigbbrothersecurity.com* – 5 July 2016].

****

CHAPTER 7
From Rights To Privileges

> Warning! This chapter may upset some of your fondest and most deep-seated prejudices. Please read it carefully.

This chapter is not subjective, but is based on objective evidence. If you have any concrete facts and evidence with which to counter it, I will be more than happy to hear from you.

How relevant is this chapter to *your* personal human rights? Hugely relevant– indeed, so relevant that its relevance cannot be exaggerated. Here is a summary of some of the main points made in this chapter:

- "Political correctness" (PC), which claims to be concerned about equality and rights, turns out in reality–on the basis of evidence – to be about special privileges for certain favoured groups.
- One major aspect of PC is feminism, which, while claiming to be concerned to achieve equality between men and women, actually ends up demanding special privileges for women.
- It is important to note that not all women are taken in by the PC line.
- Two noteworthy exceptions (among many) who are mentioned in this chapter are Ann Widdecombe and Baroness Deech.

- Ann Widdecombe, a long-serving Member of Parliament (from 1987 to 2010), has come out openly and vocally against all-women shortlists for Parliamentary elections, commenting that the Suffragettes who had fought for equal voting rights for women "wanted equal opportunities not special privileges and would have thrown themselves under the King's horse to protest against positive discrimination and all-women shortlists".
- All-women shortlists and quotas, as Ann Widdecombe has stressed, amount to discrimination, which is exactly what PC is supposed to be against.
- All-women shortlists also happen to be undemocratic. They were challenged -- ironically enough -- by the Equal Opportunities Commission and were found to be illegal by a unanimous Industrial Tribunal in 1996 as being contrary to the Sex Discrimination Act 1975.
- Baroness Deech, the former head of the Bar Standards Board and Principal of St Anne's College, Oxford, has repeatedly urged that the divorce laws are "urgently in need of reform". She says that the divorce laws should be tougher on women, because the law as interpreted now encourages them to shun work and "find a footballer to marry" instead. In the words of Baroness Deech: "We have a whole area of law which says once you [the woman] are married you need never go out to work, [that] you are automatically entitled to

everything you might need even if that marriage breaks down and it's your fault."
- The chapter assembles scientific evidence on the differences between males and females.
- The victimization of Professor Larry Summers, a distinguished economist and President of Harvard University, and of Sir Tim Hunt, a medical Nobel prizewinner, is well documented.
- The arguments in favour of prenuptial agreements -- which can assist women as well as men -- have been accepted by the Law Commission, and Baroness Deech has introduced a Bill in the House of Lords to make prenuptial agreements binding.

As you can see, all these points are extremely relevant to *your* human rights, whether you are male or female. If you are male, *your* human rights at work, as a student, as a husband or as a voter are not only under threat: they have already been depleted. And if you are female, do you really want to owe your advantages to reverse discrimination? Wouldn't you prefer to make your way on the basis of genuine competition and merit? Here are a few examples of the practical ways that the recent escalation of PC feminism affects *your* rights:

- o **Employment**: In 2014 the UK Cabinet Office announced the policy of increasing the percentage of women in senior civil service and top management posts to 39% and 34% respectively within 5 years. This has nothing to do with merit, but is based solely on numbers. This is reverse discrimination in favour of women and against men.

- **Students:** University College London has dropped its requirement of Maths and Physics A-Levels for Civil Engineering in order to attract more female students – who are then given extra lessons in Maths once they are admitted. This is privilege for those (female) students and discrimination against the male students who would otherwise have been admitted.
- **Divorce:** It is widely recognized that divorce is unfair to me. (See above). The recent case of Graham Mills, who is having to pay for his wife's financial mistakes 15 years after their divorce, is just the latest of a long line of similar cases. It was front-page news in the Evening Standard on 8 February 2017, showing that the outrage at this unjust decision is widely shared. Is this about rights? That's precisely what it's about.
- **Prenuptial agreements** are recognized in America and in most European countries. Their purpose is to protect the wealth of both parties in the event of a divorce. But as the man usually has to support the woman, he is more likely to benefit from a prenup. In the UK only one prenuptial

agreement has been approved – even though the Law Commission favours them. (See above).
- o **Democratic rights:** Women-only lists for Parliament are undemocratic and were ruled by an Industrial Tribunal to be illegal under the Sex Discrimination Act – in a case brought by the Equal Opportunities Commission! It directly affects the rights not only of men who want to stand for Parliament but also of voters.

Starting as a faintly comical word-game, "political correctness" (PC) has become the dominant ethos in the West, covering not just language but also thought and conduct. It has gained a stranglehold over the "chattering classes" in Britain, America and Western Europe who dominate the universities, the courts, the media and the entertainment industry and also have a major influence in politics and government. It is a bastardized form of liberalism and employs liberal language and labels, notably "human rights", "equality", "non-discrimination", "rule of law" and "democracy". Its adherents are quite likely to be genuine believers in these liberal values, but when those values fail to materialize in practice they become distorted. In particular, the ideal of equal rights for all tends to degenerate in practice into special privileges for some.

Human and civil rights originated in order to replace privilege with equality, in the French Revolution for example.

When this objective of equality fails to materialize, the

most usual solution is to resort to forced non-discrimination, then to positive or reverse discrimination or affirmative action, and then to quotas, which are a form of privilege. So what began as a right becomes a privilege – back to square one!

Racial Discrimination

The opposition to racial discrimination in the United States is a good example of this. Abraham Lincoln's Emancipation Proclamation of 1863 followed by three constitutional amendments gave African Americans the same legal rights in the US as Whites. In practice, however, this was not so. In the landmark decision of *Plessy v. Ferguson* (1896) the U.S. Supreme Court approved the doctrine of "separate but equal," upholding the constitutionality of racial segregation in public facilities. This decision was overturned in *Brown v. Board of Education* (1954), which decided that "separate educational facilities are inherently unequal" – ushering in an era of enforced desegregation including forced busing (introduced in 1971).

When these attempts at enforced equality failed, resort was had to quotas (subsequently struck down) and other forms of affirmative action, which effectively turned Black students into a privileged minority. Clarence Thomas, the only Black justice on the US Supreme Court, placed a sticker marked "15 cents" on his diploma from Yale, to which he had been admitted as a result of affirmative action. He explains it like this: "I'd graduated from one of America's top law schools, but racial preference had robbed my achievement of its true value." How different is the position in the UK?

Theresa May: "Blacks treated more harshly by Criminal Justice System."
In her first statement as Prime Minister on 13 July 2016, Theresa May roundly declared: *"If you're black, you're treated more harshly by the criminal justice system than if you're white."* The same sweeping statement was repeated word for word in a speech delivered at the Charity Commission on 9 January 2017 – by which time Theresa May had been Prime Minister for almost six months. This is part of Theresa May's attempt to rebrand herself and her government as in some sense "liberal". In so doing, is Theresa May here not condemning her own government as well as that of her failed predecessor, David Cameron, under whom Theresa May served as Home Secretary for six years? Such sweeping admissions are rare among politicians, and Theresa May was presumably hoping to win the plaudits of the "liberal" or even the "politically correct" establishment.

Theresa May's sweeping statement appears at first sight to be supported by official government statistics, notably a publication in the "National Statistics" series titled Statistics on Race and the Criminal Justice System 2014, published by the Ministry of Justice on 26 November 2015, the Executive Summary of which asserts: "in general, Black, Asian and Minority Ethnic (BAME) groups appear to be over-represented at most stages throughout the Criminal Justice

System, compared with the White ethnic group, though this is not universal and does not appear to increase as they progress through the Criminal Justice System." [page 7]. We also read: "Relative to the population, the Black ethnic group had the highest rate of prosecutions. The rate of prosecutions for the Black ethnic group was three times higher than for the White group. The Mixed group had the second highest rate, which was 2 times higher than the White group, while Chinese and Others had the lowest rate of prosecutions."

However, the detailed statistics contained in the body of the report tell a very different story. Violence against the person offences: "White offenders had a conviction ratio that was 8 percentage points higher than BAME offenders." The figures (as shown on a barchart) are: approximately 70% for Whites, approximately 55% for Black – with all BAME well under 60%.

The figures for conviction rates for all indictable offences show a White conviction ratio of over 80%, and BAME well under 80% [Fig 5.05]. (These ratios are annoyingly shown only in barcharts without precise figures).

So, even though a higher proportion of Blacks was prosecuted than Whites, of those prosecuted, a higher percentage of Whites was convicted (about 70%) than Blacks (about 55%). Theresa May's sweeping condemnation of the Criminal Justice System will simply not stand up to scrutiny.

Theresa May will presumably want to follow up her fallacious conclusion about Black victimization by giving Blacks special privileges in the Criminal Justice System.

Fortunately, however, this is likely to remain bombast rather than action, if it matches her dismal failure to control non-EU migration as Home Secretary.

"Political Correctness" and Special Privileges

"Political Correctness" seeks to right the wrongs done to any group or element in society that is perceived as suffering discrimination or is regarded as in any sense the "underdog". Hence the favour in the form of special privileges shown to minorities, women, gays, "trans" people and those suffering from disabilities. The courts also tend to favour other special interest groups whose claims to preferential treatment are much harder to understand – including terror suspects, asylum seekers and even convicted killers. In a rare admission, Lord Neuberger, President of the UK Supreme Court, speaking of judges in general, remarked in an address on "Fairness in the court: the best we can do", to the Criminal Justice Alliance on 10 April 2015: "I dare say that we all suffer from a degree of unconscious bias...." The "unconscious bias" that he was thinking of seems to be against people who are poor, foreign or uneducated, which is strange, because the "unconscious bias" that is most obvious in court judgments (though not in Lord Neuberger's own judgments) is a bias in favour of the special interest groups listed above.

Feminism and Privilege

In his hard-hitting book *The Myth of Male Power* (1993), Warren Farrell showed just how false the common perception of male power is: "We don't call the one million men who were killed or maimed in one battle in World War I (the battle of the Somme) a holocaust, we call it 'serving the country'. We don't call those who selected only men to die 'murderers'. We call them 'voters'." Posters displayed in Post Offices across the United States during the Vietnam War screamed: "A Man's Gotta Do What a Man's Gotta Do." And what was it that a man had "gotta" do? Why, register for the draft of course and be prepared to give up his life in a senseless and unwinnable conflict. At least 58,000 American service personnel -- overwhelmingly male -- were killed in that futile exercise. This peremptorily worded poster was a successor to the famous British World War I poster showing Lord Kitchener pointing an accusatory finger – only at males: "Your Country Needs You." That was before the introduction of conscription. With a sense of duty so ingrained in the male psyche, thousands of young men volunteered, and many teenage boys even falsified their age so as to be eligible to be slaughtered in the trenches often just a few weeks later.

During World War I women evidently had no compunction about sending young men to their death. Some women would even make a habit of patrolling the streets and shaming with a white feather -- the badge of cowardice -- any mere male who was not in uniform, as if to say: "Go and die for me: my life is more valuable than yours."

The main justification for confining military call-up exclusively to males is of course that they are on average physically stronger than females and also that they are less likely to be caring for young children. Females are still commonly treated by males in the West as tender flowers requiring delicate handling and special respect. Traditionally, this entailed men opening doors for women, raising their hats to them, giving up their seats to them on a bus or train, and even getting up as soon as a woman entered the room. This kind of chivalry has declined with the rise of the feminist movement, which has inadvertently shown up the anomaly between treating women with kid gloves and treating them as equals. But this anomaly still persists, with women expecting preferential treatment at the same time as demanding equal rights – or, rather, for special privileges.

Male/Female Brain Connectivity

There is no shortage of anecdotal evidence contrasting males and females, but what is the true situation? A report by ten scientists attached to the University of Pennsylvania on male/female brain connectivity published in 2013 in the peer-reviewed *Proceedings of the National Academy of Sciences* contained the following findings:

- Males' brains are on average 11% to 12% bigger than females' brains.
- In females there is strong wiring between the left and right hemispheres, "suggesting that they facilitate communication between the analytical and intuition".
- In males, by contrast, there is greater neural connectivity from front to back and within each

hemisphere, "suggesting that their brains are structured to facilitate connectivity between perception and coordinated action."

These findings, based on a study of 949 subjects between the ages of 8 and 22, support stereotypes observed formally and informally over a long period of time, such as:

- Males tend to be more logical and better at coordination than females;
- Males tend to be better at mathematics than females. The inferior-parietal lobule (IPL), which is thought to control mathematical ability, tends to be significantly larger in males than in females. This area of Albert Einstein's brain was found to be abnormally large;
- Males tend to be better at map-reading than females – as generations of infuriated males have found when driving with a female navigator sitting next to them;
- Females tend to have better linguistic skills than males – a feature that is noticeable in children as young as four years old;
- Females tend to be more intuitive than males and have greater "emotional intelligence";
- Females tend to be better than males at multi-tasking –the subject of countless jokes.

Nobody objects when males are ridiculed for their perceived shortcomings compared to females, but political correctness kicks in the moment there is a whiff of a suggestion that women may be less good than men in any respect. The case of the liberal economist Larry Summers who was forced to resign as President of Harvard University because of a (highly guarded) remark about females in science and engineering is just the tip of the iceberg. Larry Summers' very tentative breach of the feminism code, which cost him his position as President of Harvard and also his likely appointment as US Treasury Secretary, is only one of the better-known examples. And what was Professor Summers' unforgivable sin? At a conference in 2005 he had the temerity to put forward three alternative hypotheses on why women were outnumbered by men in high-end science and engineering positions. One of these hypotheses explained the difference partly at least in terms of innate differences in ability or preferences between men and women. This set off a firestorm, as a result of which, despite Summers' repeated apologies, he was virtually forced to resign as President of Harvard. This incident is shocking in two different ways: first, by revealing the precarious nature of freedom of speech, or even of academic freedom in general, at a leading university; and secondly, as an example of PC denial of the possibility of natural differences between the sexes.

Nobel Prizewinner Censured Over "Sexist" Remark

Professor Sir Tim Hunt, a medical Nobel prizewinner, was similarly forced to resign as an honorary professor at University College, London (UCL), for making a "sexist" remark. The offending remark was this lighthearted comment, made at an international conference in Seoul, South Korea: "Let me tell you about my trouble with girls...three things happen when they are in the lab...You fall in love with them, they fall in love with you, and when you criticise them they cry. Perhaps we should make separate labs for boys and girls?" The university's po-faced reply published on their website welcomed the Nobel laureate's resignation, adding: "UCL was the first university in England to admit women students on equal terms to men, and the university believes that this outcome is compatible with our commitment to gender equality" – a classic PC response. Sir Tim Hunt apologized for any offence, saying that he meant the remarks to be humorous – but adding that he "did mean the part about having trouble with girls". [*The Guardian*, 11 June 2015]. Why was his remark so offensive? Presumably because of his attribution to females of an overly emotional reaction to criticism – a stereotype which was obviously not meant to apply to *all* females but which will ring a bell with many males who have worked with females in many different walks of life.

Maths & Physics

In Britain only about 20% of students opting to take A-Level Physics are female. Physics and Mathematics A-Levels are generally prerequisite entry criteria for Engineering degree courses. In 2006, when only 21% of students in the Civil, Environmental and Geomatic Engineering department of

University College, London, were female, the department decided to change their entry requirements in order to attract more female students. Since then, Maths and Physics A-Levels have no longer been required for admission to the course – but applicants accepted without a Maths A-Level are given extra Maths lessons to catch up. As a result of the new policy, female students in the department in 2015 accounted for 29% of the total. A female student accepted without a Maths or Physics A-Level confided in a 2015 interview: "I found the Maths really hard, I won't lie." And, referring to the extra Maths lessons, added: "That support especially coming up to exams was really invaluable." [*Evening Standard*, 22 April 2015].

So, even after going to all this trouble, the proportion of female students on the course was still less than a third, but the university apparently hopes to increase the number of female students to 50%. The real question is: why is it necessary to adopt a quota system? This is all part of the PC insistence on the equality of the sexes. Feminists tend to attribute the differences to social conditioning making girls prefer to play with dolls while boys prefer to play with Lego or Meccano sets. But these stereotypes are obviously not the result of social conditioning: they are *natural* – a dirty word among the PC brigade.

Computer Science

A good indication of the naturalness of this tendency is the low proportion of females interested in computer science.

Computing is such a recent development that there simply has not been enough time to develop an IT "culture" associated with either gender. But from the outset boys took quite naturally to computing, while girls tended to show much less interest. In fact, the percentage of female Computer Science graduates has actually declined over the past thirty years. The percentage of female Computer Science graduates in the US peaked at 37% in 1985, but was down to 18% by 2014 and 14% at top research universities. [Readwrite.com, September 2, 2014]. And at the time of writing fewer than a quarter of the jobs in the IT industry across the world are held by women.

As with the small number of females in engineering, this is considered to be a major problem – which it is from a PC perspective but not otherwise. This non-problem is particularly embarrassing to the PC brigade, who, in the absence of a longstanding traditional male culture to blame it on, have to fall back on allegations of sexual discrimination, macho organizational culture or lack of "encouragement" for girls to go into IT. The real reason for low female participation in IT is quite simple. Computer Science is highly mathematical and abstract, making it more attractive to the typical male brain than to the average female brain. In other words, low female interest in Computer Science is natural.

The "Glass Ceiling"
What is even more galling to the PC brigade than the disparity between the number of males and females in engineering and

IT is the supposed gap between male and female earnings and the so-called "glass ceiling". As of April 2016 it was loudly complained that in the US a woman was paid 79 cents for every dollar paid to a man. However, data published in 2008 showed that single childless women aged between 22 and 30 were actually earning more than their male counterparts in most US cities, with incomes that were on average 8% higher than those of the males. [Dougherty, Conor, "Young Women's Pay Exceeds Male Peers", *Wall Street Journal*, Sept 1, 2010].

These figures revealing higher earning females are not at all well known. On the contrary, the PC brigade continues to scream "discrimination" in regard to the 79-cent disparity, the "glass ceiling" and any other examples that they can find where males appear to be favoured over females.

The 79-cent figure has itself been challenged, as is pointed out in an excellently sourced article by Guy Bentley titled "Equal Pay Day Revisited: Why the Gender Pay Gap is Still a Myth" [dailycaller.com–12 April 2016]. Guy Bentley reports that when President Obama claimed in 2012 that women were paid only 77 cents on the dollar for doing the same work as men, Politfact labeled his statement as "mostly false".

Mark Perry, a professor of economics and finance at the University of Michigan and an economist at the American Enterprise Institute, writes: "The American Association of University Women (AAUW), along with the National Committee on Pay Equity (NCPE), are major participants in the feminist propaganda machine that mobilizes its forces every April and engages in statistical misrepresentations to publicize the annual feminist holiday known as Equal Pay Day. Last April, AAUW executive director Linda D. Hallman sent a mass email that made this verifiably false statement (emphasis added): 'Think about it: *Women have to work almost four months longer than men do to earn the same amount of money for doing the same job.* What's more, we have to set aside a day each year just to call the nation's attention to it.' The reality is that you can only find a 23% gender pay gap by comparing raw, aggregate, unadjusted full-time median salaries, i.e. when you control for NOTHING that would help explain gender differences in salaries like:

1. **Hours Worked**: The average man working full-time worked almost two more hours per week in 2014 compared to the average woman. And the US Bureau of Labor Statistics found that women were 2.5 times more likely to have a shorter average workweek than men.

2. **Type of Work**: An important factor in the apparent pay disparity between men and women is attributable to career choice. A US Department of Labor study published in 2009 summarizing over 50 peer-reviewed papers concluded that the wage gap "may be almost entirely the result of individual choices being made by both male and female workers. Men represented 92.3% of workplace fatalities in 2014 because men far outnumber women in the most dangerous, but higher-paying occupations like logging, mining and roofing that have the greatest probability of job-related injury or death. In contrast, women, more than men, show a demonstrated preference for lower risk occupations with

greater workplace safety and comfort, and they are frequently willing to accept lower wages for the greater safety and reduced probability of work-related injury or death." [Mark Perry–www.aei.org]. One might also mention construction work generally, working on oil rigs and other outdoor occupations exposing them to extremes of temperature both hot and cold, not to mention such hazardous occupations as law enforcement, the armed forces and the fire service.

3. **Marriage and Motherhood**: (a) single women who have never married earned nearly 94% of male earnings in 2014 (but that **does not control for anything else** like hours worked, age, experience, education, occupation, children, etc); (b) more women than men leave the workforce temporarily for child birth, child care and elder care, and (c) women, especially working mothers, tend to value 'family friendly' workplace policies more than men, according to a Department of Labor study.

"Most economic studies that control for all of those variables conclude that gender discrimination accounts for only a very small fraction of gender pay differences, and may not even be a statistically significant factor at all." [Mark Perry, ibid].

No Love in Tennis
A recent furor was set off by a remark made by Ray Moore, CEO of the Indian Wells Tennis Garden, that female tennis players should "go down on their knees and thank God that

Roger Federer and Rafa Nadal were born because they have carried this sport. They really have." Needless to say, this ill-advised remark sparked off a full-scale row on the gender gap in tennis players' earnings, with Novak Djokovic weighing in with the remark that: "Stats are showing that we have much more spectators on the men's tennis matches. I think that is one of the reasons why maybe we should get awarded more." But even this outspoken sportsman soon found himself forced to kowtow to political correctness, apologizing for his remark as the product of "euphoria and adrenalin" after his Indian Wells victory! [*The Guardian*, 21 March 2016].

Yet Djokovic's remarks make perfect sense. Besides the fact that female tennis tournaments are based on a three-set rather than a five-set format, the real question is: if female tennis players are equal to their male counterparts, why don't they compete with male players? The plain fact is that female tennis is simply not in the same league as male tennis. And the same applies to most other sports as well.

Women in Parliament

In Britain there has long been pressure among the "chattering classes" for more women in Parliament. In 1993, after polls indicated that women were less likely than men to vote Labour, the Labour Party approved the policy of all-women shortlists. In 1996 an Industrial Tribunal held that all-women shortlists were illegal under the Sex Discrimination Act 1975. Despite this, in 1997 the Labour Party used all-women shortlists in no fewer than half of all winnable seats. After a reduced number of women were returned as Members of Parliament (MPs) in the 2001 general election, Tony Blair's Labour government introduced the Sex Discrimination (Election Candidates) Act 2002 allowing parties to use positive discrimination in the selection of parliamentary candidates. This provision is valid until the year 2030.

The policy of all-women shortlists has been controversial from the start, and it remains so. It beggars belief that a policy that is so blatantly discriminatory could possibly be considered democratic. Ann Widdecombe, a Conservative MP, commented in 2008 that women like the Suffragettes who had fought for equal voting rights "wanted equal opportunities not special privileges and would have thrown themselves under the King's horse to protest against positive discrimination and all-women shortlists" – a reference to the militant suffragette Emily Davison, who was killed when she stepped in front of the King's horse at the Derby in 1913. Ann Widdecombe's remark pinpoints the fundamental unfairness of all-women shortlists – that they create not equality of opportunity but privilege. This is a feature of all quotas, of which all-women shortlists are an example, and this is why the US Supreme Court has rejected quotas even while allowing other forms of affirmative action, especially in regard to Black university admissions.

The hypocrisy of the UK's so-called Government Equalities Office, set up in 2007 to promote gender equality, came to light as the result of a Freedom of Information request made by Dominic Raab MP in 2011. The enquiry revealed that female staff at the Equalities Office received on average 7.7% more pay than male staff, and that 65% of the department's 107 staff were female. Dominic Raab commented pointedly: "It undermines the credibility of the equality and diversity agenda if bureaucrats at the government equalities office are preaching about unequal representation and the pay gap whilst practicing the reverse. It smacks of double standards." [*Daily Mail*, 16 June 2011; *Daily Telegraph* 14 June 2011; *Wikipedia*, "Government Equalities Office"].

Recent British Prime Ministers have been trying to outdo one another in the number of women that they have appointed to ministerial positions. Theresa May's lacklustre administration, appointed in 2016, contained 28 female ministers as against 30 in the David Cameron administration which it replaced. Ten of the 30 ministers attending Cabinet in Cameron's final administration were female, as against 8 out of 27 (or 22 full Cabinet members) under Theresa May. These figures had nothing to do with ability, but were dictated purely by gender politics.

It is a good sign, though, that Philip Davies, an outspoken anti-feminist Member of Parliament, was recently elected unopposed to fill a Conservative place on the House of Commons Women and Equalities Committee. The MP for Shipley claimed in a speech at a conference organized by the Justice for Men and Boys party (J4MB): "Feminist zealots really do want women to have their cake and eat it. They fight for their version of equality on all the things that suit women

– but are very quick to point out that women need special protections and treatment on other things. For example, we hear plenty about increasing the numbers of women on company boards and female representation in Parliament; however, there's a deafening silence when it comes to increasing the number of men who have custody of their children or who have careers as midwives. In fact, generally there seems to be a deafening silence on all the benefits women have compared to men...I don't believe there's an issue between men and women. The problem is being stirred up by those who can be described as militant feminists and the politically correct males who pander to this nonsense." [*The Guardian* – 12 August 2016].

Marriage and Divorce

Opposition to *Roe v. Wade* has come chiefly from the pro-life movement, which believes that life begins at conception, so that the decision in *Roe* has ridden roughshod over the rights of the unborn child. But what about the rights of the father? Since *Roe v. Wade* some states in the US have passed laws requiring the husband's consent to an abortion in the case of a married woman. All these laws have been ruled unconstitutional. In *Planned Parenthood v. Danforth* (1976) the US Supreme Court struck down a Missouri law requiring prior written consent to an abortion from a parent in the case of a minor and from a husband in the case of a married woman. In *Planned Parenthood v. Casey* (1992) the Court struck down even a provision in a Pennsylvania law simply requiring a wife to *notify* her husband that she was about to have an abortion. So much for equal rights between men and women!

In Britain, where abortion was legalized by Parliament instead of being left to the courts, there has been surprisingly little acrimony, except right at the start. Unlike *Roe v. Wade* in America, it does not allow abortion on demand but it also excludes the father from any say. [See more on this in Chapter 1].

Baroness Deech: Divorce laws "urgently in need of reform"

In other respects feminism is as rampant in Britain as in America, if not more so. As originally enacted in 1970, section 5(1) of the Matrimonial Proceedings & Property Act 1970 contained a tailpiece telling the courts what their objective should be when making financial provision orders and property adjustment orders in a divorce. Courts were to exercise these powers "so as to place the parties, so far as it is practicable and having regard to their conduct, just to do so, in the financial position in which they would have been if the marriage had not broken down...." This is coded language for telling the court to give the woman half her ex-husband's income after the divorce. But this early PC feminist provision, passed in the dying days of Harold Wilson's Labour government, was swept away under a Conservative government in 1973, which however gave no guidance to the courts on how to divide up the matrimonial property. With the rise of an ever-increasing PC judiciary, the courts continue to favour the woman in divorce settlements. But a former head of the English Bar Standards Board, Baroness Deech, says that the divorce laws are "urgently in need of reform". [*Financial Times*, 30 December 2014]. She is quoted as remarking that Britain's divorce laws should be tougher on women because the law as interpreted encourages them to shun work and "find a footballer to marry" instead. "We have a whole area of law which says once you [the woman] are married you need never go out to work, [that] you are automatically entitled to everything you might need even if that marriage breaks down and it's your fault." [Quoted in *Daily Mail*, 24 February, 2015].

It is amusing to find a 2015 Court of Appeal decision hailed as a "game-changer" and "landmark ruling" simply because it rejected a millionaire's ex-wife's claim for maintenance of £75,000 a year and instead ordered her to "get a job". The decision was certainly less lopsidedly anti-husband than most English divorce rulings, but still gave the wife a large slice of the pie. (*Wright v. Wright* [2015] EWCA Civ 201). A closer look at the ruling in this divorce, between Tracey Wright and prominent racehorse surgeon Ian Wright, reveals the following:

- The 7-bedroom family home worth £1.3 million was sold after the divorce in 2008 and the proceeds divided equally between husband and wife.
- The order did not cut the wife off to fend for herself. Instead, she was to receive declining amounts from £32,000 a year to

£24,000 a year and then £12,000 a year, with maintenance ceasing only at the end of 2019, when the husband was due to retire.
- In addition, the husband had to continue to pay child maintenance of £20,400 a year until both his daughters reach the age of 17, plus their private school fees.
- The wife had been told at the time of the divorce in 2008 to be prepared to find work, but she had not done so, so this message was finally repeated by the court in 2015.

Although the Wright case marks a welcome departure from the long line of English cases in which the ex-husband was ordered to pay maintenance for the rest of his life or until his ex-wife remarried, that unfair approach is purely the invention of PC English judges, who will doubtless continue to apply it, treating the Wright case as turning on its own exceptional facts.

Since writing the previous paragraph I have unfortunately been proved right by events. On 8 February 2017 the *Evening Standard* ran a front-page news story headed: "It's time to end divorce payouts for life." The case involved a decision by the Court of Appeal under which the former husband, Graham Mills was ordered to pay his ex-wife £1,441 a month – up from the £1,000 a month originally ordered when the couple were divorced in 2002 after 13 years of marriage. In addition to these monthly personal maintenance payments the ex-wife had received a £230,000 lump sum. The reason for the increased award was that the ex-wife, a former estate agent, had fallen "heavily into debt after investing 'unwisely' in a series of ever more 'upmarket' London properties in a bid to climb the housing ladder" and was now "unable to meet her basic needs". [*The Telegraph*, 6 February 2017]. "I don't think it's right that after divorce you should be tied together forever," commented Graham Mills. "I feel like I am paying for her mismanagement of finances." [*Evening Standard*, 8 February 2017]. The ruling means that Mr Mills has now been supporting his ex-wife for 15 years -- two years longer than the whole time that they were married -- with no end in sight. It is time Parliament acted by legislating to stop this kind of injustice.

Other Jurisdictions

It is important to realize that the PC anti-male attitude of the English courts goes well beyond what we find in most other jurisdictions. Even in Scotland the typical English approach to divorce would be unthinkable. The position in certain other countries is as follows:

- Scotland – maintenance for a maximum of three years;
- Spain – maintenance generally for a maximum of two years;
- Germany – an ex-wife looking after children is expected to go (back) to work once the youngest turns three.

The American courts do tend to favour the wife over the husband, but the salvation of wealthy American men -- and women -- is the prenuptial agreement, or "prenup", which can be used to ring-fence the assets belonging to the wealthier partner -- almost invariably the husband -- and limit the amount of alimony he will have to pay in the event of a divorce.

Prenuptial Agreements

In England prenuptial agreements are not generally recognized. The one case where it has been recognized was -- surprise, surprise! -- one which happened to protect the wife! The German heiress Katrin Radmacher signed a prenup with her husband, Nicolas Granatino, which stipulated that neither party would have a financial claim on the other if they got divorced. But it was only when the case got to the UK Supreme Court in 2010 that the prenup was recognized. (*Radmacher v. Granatino* [2010] UKSC 42). Contrary to comment at the time, this decision does not mark a sea-change in the approach of the English courts. In a rambling judgment the majority on the Supreme Court held that "In future it will be natural to infer that parties entering into an ante-nuptial agreement to which English law is likely to be applied intend that effect should be given to it." However, that does not amount to recognizing prenuptial or ante-nuptial agreements as legally enforceable contracts. The Supreme Court made it clear that a prenup would only be recognized "in the right case" and that the courts still retained the discretion to ignore a prenup if they wished.

"Some lawyers," it was reported, "claimed that the landmark decision represented a constitutional upset in which judges had started making rather than interpreting the law." [Owen Bowcott in *The Guardian*, 20 October 2010]. It is quite right that the true role of judges is not to make law but merely to interpret it. But recognizing the validity of a prenuptial agreement is not making law but merely applying the ordinary principles of contract law. Provided the two parties enter into the agreement of their own free will, a prenup should be as binding a contract as marriage itself – which of course is a contract too. One objection that has been raised to prenups is that they lack what we lawyers call *consideration* – or a quid pro quo. For example, in most commercial contracts one party provides goods or services in return for payment provided by the other party. In the case of a prenup, the consideration for agreeing to the prenup is surely entry into the marriage contract. Because, if a party refuses to sign a prenup, the wedding is off! So the remark on the Radmacher case attributed to "some lawyers" is exactly the opposite of the truth. It is precisely when they refuse to recognize prenups that judges are overstepping their true constitutional role and are making law rather than interpreting it. Why, after all, are prenups recognized in so many other countries, notably of course throughout the United States, but also in many European countries, including France and Germany? Answer: because they have all the ingredients required for a binding contract.

An experienced female solicitor was quoted as commenting on the Radmacher decision: "This decision could introduce an inherent degree of sex discrimination within the family court system as prenuptial agreements predominantly benefit the rich and it is more commonly the woman in the marriage who is the financially weaker party." [Quoted *The Guardian* 20 October 2010]. In fact, however, recognition of prenuptial agreements will not introduce sex discrimination into the system – it will do the exact opposite. It will serve to correct the discrimination -- against husbands -- that is already prevalent. One can but wonder if the Radmacher case itself would have been decided the way it was if the wealthier partner seeking to protect their assets by enforcing a prenup had been the husband!

In 2014 the Law Commission, an advisory body, published a lengthy report on prenuptial agreements titled *Matrimonial Property Needs & Agreements*. The report concludes: "We recommend statutory confirmation of the contractual validity of marital property agreements – which sounds positive, but is immediately followed by this qualification: "they will be upheld, only if they are 'not unfair', in accordance with the decision of the Supreme Court in *Radmacher v. Granatino*." The report appends a draft "Nuptial Agreements Bill" which repeats this nullifying exception and has not been passed into law in any event.

Neither the government nor the opposition has taken the badly needed and far from revolutionary step of introducing legislation giving legal recognition to prenuptial agreements.

Baroness Deech (quoted above) has herself bravely introduced a private member's Bill in the House of Lords, titled Divorce (Financial Provisions) Bill, which has not been passed, providing that "a pre-nuptial or post-nuptial agreement is to be treated as binding", unless the parties failed to obtain independent legal advice beforehand, unless the agreement was made less than 21 days before the marriage, and unless there was full prior disclosure of assets between the parties. So far so good. But the Bill then adds a further negative condition preventing a prenuptial or post-nuptial agreement from being treated as unenforceable "unless the agreement is unenforceable under the rules of contract law." This rider effectively scuppers the whole Bill, because, as the Radmacher case indicated, the UK Supreme Court is not prepared to recognize prenuptial agreements as binding contracts. This underlines the serious plight that English law finds itself in, some aspects of which are as follows:

- English Common Law contains settled principles of contract law which determine whether a particular agreement qualifies as a binding contract or not.
- Prenuptial agreements do qualify as binding contracts under these principles (see above).
- However, the English courts have arrogated to themselves the right to depart from these principles and, in so doing, refuse to recognize prenuptial agreements as binding contracts.

- The principles of the Common Law go back centuries, but in many jurisdictions, like the great majority of states of the US, these principles have been codified, or in other words, enacted as legislation passed in each case by the state legislature concerned with the consent of the state governor.
- It is not for the courts or the judges to make up the principles of the Common Law. By doing so they are overstepping the bounds of their power, which is merely to interpret and apply the principles.
- However, where the courts raise doubts about the principles of the Common Law, as has happened in regard to prenuptial agreements, it is time for Parliament, under the leadership of the Government, to step in and enact these principles as legislation.

****

CHAPTER 8
Your Right To A Fair Trial

This important right, or bundle of rights, is protected by ECHR Article 6 together with an uncoordinated slew of statutory rights. Article 6 covers civil as well as criminal trials, but criminal defendants are accorded several additional protections, including the presumption of innocence, the right to legal representation together with the right to call witnesses and examine witnesses called by the prosecution.

The existence of these rights largely depends on some major principles, which exist more in the realm of hype than in practice:

a) The Rule of Law;
b) Equality before the Law; and
c) Natural Justice.

Let's look at each of these in turn:

The Rule of Law – The American founding father John Adams, who was to become the second president of the USA, coined this principle, which (in slightly modified form) was incorporated into the Massachusetts Constitution of 1780: "A

Government not of men but of laws". But a wag immediately retorted: "A government not of laws but of lawyers." The cheeky wag was right. Laws cannot rule. They are just words on paper (if that). They need to be interpreted and applied – which is the function of the courts. But in so doing, it is the courts who are ruling and not the laws, especially if the judges stray from interpreting the law into making law, which is the province of Parliament. Lord Denning, probably the best-known UK judge of the 20th century, had to be told off repeatedly for what Viscount Simonds in 1950 called "a naked usurpation of the legislative function under the thin disguise of interpretation". But Lord Denning's judicial activism or judicial supremacism (though not his mastery of the old law reports) has had many emulators. In a 2015 lawsuit about the media's access to Prince Charles's letters to the then Prime Minister, decided by a 5-2 majority in the UK Supreme Court, the two dissenting justices bravely impugned the whole basis of the majority decision. The majority, held Lord Wilson, "did not in my view interpret section 53 of the Freedom of Information Act 2000. It re-wrote it. It invoked precious constitutional principles, but among the most precious is that of parliamentary sovereignty, emblematic of our democracy." The other brave dissenter, Lord Hughes, similarly disparaged the majority's mistaken understanding of the concept of the rule of law: "The rule of law is of the first importance. But it is an integral part of the rule of law that courts give effect to Parliamentary intention. The rule of law is not the same as a rule that courts must always prevail, no matter what the statute says." [*R (Evans) v. Attorney General* [2015] UKSC 21]. The danger of giving the judges a free hand to interpret the laws as they liked was identified by King James I four hundred years ago: "If the judges interpret the laws themselves and suffer none else to interpret, they may easily make, of the laws, shipmen's hose!" [*Prohibitions del Roy, or Case of Prohibitions* [1607] EWHC KBJ23] -- meaning that judge-made law would come to resemble the tattered and frayed stockings worn by sailors -- a pretty good description of English law 400 years later.

Equality before the Law

Equality before the law is always considered to be an absolute prerequisite for democracy and also for "the rule of law". But does it really exist?

There are several problem areas:

- **Affordability**: "The law courts are open to all – just like the Ritz Hotel." This is an oft-quoted remark originally made by a facetious Victorian judge, the point being that, except in the most nominal sense, the Ritz is not really open to all, as its prices are prohibitive to all but the well-heeled. This is still largely true of the law courts, and even the availability of no-win-no-fee legal representation (which applies only to claimants and then only in cases approved by solicitors offering this service) does not really solve the problem.

- **Access to Justice**: The right to access to justice is only touched on in ECHR Article 6 in regard to legal representation, including a provision that a criminal defendant is to be given free legal assistance "when the interests of justice so require". Article 47 of the European Charter goes further by stipulating that "Legal aid shall be made available to those who lack sufficient resources in so far as such aid is necessary to ensure effective access to justice." In the UK legal aid for civil cases has largely dried up, and even criminal legal aid is now much reduced in scope. However, the effect (if any) of the European Charter in the UK is unclear, as the UK negotiated an opt-out protocol from it at the outset. And the Charter will in any event presumably cease to apply to the UK altogether after finalization of Brexit.
- **Civil costs:** The UK is one of the few countries in the world where bringing a claim for, say, £50,000 could end up costing you £500,000. This is because of the system under which the loser pays the winner's largely uncontrolled costs. The courts normally allow the bulk of the winner's costs to go through on the nod. Even where there is "detailed assessment" of costs, an expensive procedure which occurs in only a minority of cases, the reduction in the costs claimed by the winning party is usually quite minimal.
- **Jackson reforms:** Reforms to the civil costs regime proposed in an elaborate report prepared by Lord

Justice Jackson in 2010 resulted in the introduction of fixed costs for personal injury claims valued up to £25,000, which did not get to grips with the real problem.

- **German system:** I for one was disappointed with the very limited effect of the Jackson reforms. In a number of articles I had long advocated adoption of something similar to the German system, a statutory scheme which is fair to all concerned. Like the British system, it is based on the loser paying the winner's legal costs. But that is where the similarity ends. Unlike the British system, the German system allows a person to sue someone else without the fear of losing their house. It enables cases to be decided quickly without endless hearings, adjournments and delays (which are standard in the UK). And it enables lawyers to make a good living without being greedy. It works on a sliding scale – backwards. Before the reforms of 2013 the figures were as follows. For the lowest value cases the winner could recover costs equivalent to 20% of the value of the claim. As the value of the claim increased, so the percentage decreased, until costs equivalent to 2% of the value of the claim were recoverable for claims of more than 200,000 euros. The logic behind this fair and simple scheme is that there is a minimum amount of work that a lawyer has to do in even the smallest of cases, but the amount of work does not increase in proportion to the value of the claim. The work involved in a claim worth 100,000 euros is undoubtedly more than for a case worth 20,000 euros – but not five times as much. The German figures were revised upwards in 2013, but the basic principles of the scheme remain the same, and it is regulated by statute.www.foris.com/service-center/prozesskostenrechner.html].

- **New Jackson Proposals:** In his preliminary report, published in 2009, Lord Justice Jackson described and discussed the German system in some detail – only to dismiss it in a few lines in his final report of 2010 as not being suitable to the UK situation. When I happened to bump into Lord Justice Jackson at a conference and told him of my disappointment, he assured me of his admiration for the German system but said that it could not be introduced in the UK without the appointment of many more judges. I found this remark quite puzzling. It is true that in Germany it is usual for there to be at least three judges sitting on any case (as against the extremely unfair UK norm of having all first instance cases heard by just a single judge). But hearings in Germany are much shorter and the UK system of wasteful repeated preliminary and interlocutory hearings is unheard of.

- **Two-lawyer system:** Unlike most other countries, the UK has two legal professions: barristers and solicitors. Most people looking for a lawyer will generally go to a solicitor first, but if the case has to go to court the solicitor will generally recommend "taking counsel's opinion", and then "instructing counsel " to represent the client in court, the term "counsel" referring to a barrister. In fact, however, as is still not well known, as a member of the public you can go direct to a barrister, not only for litigation but also for legal advice and the drafting of documents in non-contentious cases as well. The advantage of this is not only that you will be paying only one lawyer instead of two but also that barristers' fees tend to be much more transparent. When you hire a solicitor you will generally be asked to sign a "retainer" agreement giving the solicitor the right to act on your behalf by writing letters or doing anything else that the solicitor considers necessary without asking you. When signing the retainer you will generally have to pay the solicitor a lump sum "on account", and you will then be billed periodically. Amazingly, solicitors do not have to provide itemized bills, though a client is entitled to request one. If you come direct to a barrister the position is quite different. For each piece of work you must instruct the barrister separately by means of a signed contract which is individually billed and usually payable in advance. So with a barrister there are no hidden fees or surprise bills: you know where you stand at every point. <u>Note</u>: I have to disclose an interest, as I am myself a Barrister who has been registered for public access since that was first introduced in 2004.

Natural Justice

Although not spelled out in ECHR Article 6, the right to a fair trial must also include the two ancient fundamental principles of natural justice:

- The rule of fairness -- *Audi alteram partem* -- literally "hear the other side", meaning that both sides in a lawsuit must be treated the same, with equal access to justice and an equal opportunity to present their case. Costs etc – see above.
- The rule against bias -- *Nemo debet esse judex in causa sua* -- literally, "Nobody ought to be a judge in his own cause (or case)".

Apparent Bias - The Pinochet Case

While on a private visit to Britain for medical treatment in 1998, the former Chilean dictator, General Augusto Pinochet, was suddenly arrested under an international arrest warrant issued by a Spanish judge alleging the torture of a number of Spanish citizens nearly twenty years earlier together with the alleged assassination of a Spanish diplomat in 1975. Senator Pinochet was placed under house arrest, initiating a hard-fought extradition battle in the UK courts. The House of Lords, then the top UK court, rejected Pinochet's claim of immunity from suit as a former head of state and by a 3-2 majority gave the go-ahead to his extradition to Spain. It turned out, however, that, Lord Hoffmann, one of the three "law lords" who voted against Pinochet, was an unpaid director and chairman of Amnesty International Charity Ltd, a charity associated with Amnesty International, a human rights organization which had been allowed to participate in the hearing as an "intervener", being represented in court by a team of four barristers, who addressed the court in favour of General Pinochet's extradition to Spain. General Pinochet's lawyers then lodged a petition asking for Lord Hoffmann's opinion to be declared invalid, or, alternatively, for the decision of the House of Lords to be set aside.

This was a completely unprecedented situation, as there was no provision for any appeal from a House of Lords decision. A fresh panel of law lords was summoned to hear this petition. Lord Hope struck a critical note: "I think that the connections which existed between Lord Hoffmann and Amnesty International were of such a character, in view of their duration and proximity, as to disqualify him on this ground.....There has been no suggestion that he was actually biased.....But his relationship with Amnesty International was such that he was, in effect, acting as a judge in his own cause. I consider that his failure to disclose these connections leads to the conclusion that the decision to which he was a party must be set aside." The House of Lords stressed that in this class of case the disqualification of the judge in question was "automatic", in which it is not necessary to show a "real danger" or even a "reasonable suspicion" of bias, let alone any actual bias on his part. [*R (Pinochet Ugarte) v. Bow Street Metropolitan Stipendiary Magistrate (No. 2)* [1999] 1 Al ER 577].

The current UK test for judicial "apparent bias" calling for the judge to recuse himself from a case is the following, as approved by the House of Lords in *Porter v. Magill* [2002] AC 357: "The court must first ascertain all the circumstances which have a bearing on the suggestion that the judge was biased. It must then ask whether those circumstances would lead a fair-minded and informed observer to conclude that there was a real possibility that the judge" or "tribunal was biased."

This is an improvement on the "real danger" and "reasonable suspicion" tests by moving away from trying to look inside the head of the judge concerned and focusing instead on the impression created by his conduct on an outside observer. But what exactly are the qualifications for a "fair-minded and informed observer"? Including this requirement as part of the test only makes it more difficult to conclude that there has been any apparent bias. Why not revert to the much simpler test proposed by that great Victorian judge, Lord Esher MR: Not only must judges not be biased, yet if the circumstances are such that people – not reasonable people but many people – would suspect them of being biased, they ought not to sit as judges." [*Eckersley v. Mersey Docks* [1891-94] All ER Rep 1130].

Problems with the Recusal Rules

Mr Justice Peter Smith, a High Court judge of the Chancery Division, provides a good example of the problems with the recusal rules. His conduct in a 2007 case was condemned by a unanimous Court of Appeal, which concluded that the judge ought to have acceded to the application made to him to recuse himself from the case in question. [*Howell v. Lees-Millais* [2007] EWCA Civ 720]. This was followed by a reprimand by the Lord Chief Justice. However, a further recusal spat occurred in 2013 with the Court of Appeal concluding that the judge should have recused himself from a specific wasted costs application. And in 2015 the same judge was presented with yet another application to recuse himself, which he eventually agreed to do. This was in a case involving British Airways, with which the judge had his own personal dispute following the loss of his luggage after a flight from Florence to London. [2015] EWHC 2201 (Ch)]. Whatever the rights and wrongs of Mr Justice Smith's conduct, his story reveals some serious problems with the relevant legal arrangements:

- Why was it initially left to the judge to decide whether to recuse himself or not?
- This is itself contrary to the rule of bias: *nemo debet esse judex in causa sua.* ["nobody ought to be a judge in his own case"].
- Some senior judges have themselves criticized the system of having to apply to the very judge who you want to stand down. In the 2015 F. A. Mann lecture Lord Neuberger approved this remark from an article by Lord Justice Sedley: "The important thing is that the system should not compound one paradox – a judge who is unbiased but might reasonably be thought not

to be – with a further paradox: a judge who, in order to decide whether he will be sitting as judge in his own cause, has to sit as judge in his own cause." [Lord Neuberger, "Judge not, that ye be not judged", F.A. Mann Lecture 2015.

- Why are there no disciplinary penalties for bias or apparent bias?
- This unsatisfactory state of affairs is yet another result of the dereliction of duty on the part of the Government and Parliament in failing to legislate for this kind of eventuality.
- In the United States this problem is neatly dealt with by statute–28 United States Code Section 144, which under the heading "Bias or prejudice of judge", provides that when a party to a case in a US District Court files a "timely and sufficient Motion that the judge before whom the matter is pending has a personal bias or prejudice either against him or in favor of an adverse party", the case must be transferred to another judge.
- There is also provision under Title 28 of United States Code section 455 for a judge to "disqualify himself in any proceeding in which his impartiality might reasonably be questioned". And even US Supreme Court justices have on occasion recused themselves of their own accord from hearing a particular case. A judge is expected to recuse himself where there are grounds for him to do so. A judge who does not do so

when he knows or ought to know that such grounds exist may be subject to sanctions.
- Why can't the UK follow the sensible and practical US system? The UK system (if it even merits that description) is messy and, by handing the initial decision to the judge in question himself, breaches one of the most fundamental principles of natural justice – and, if the judge concerned is recalcitrant, this arrangement can easily create an unseemly row.

"Unconscious Bias"

In a rare admission the President of the UK Supreme Court, Lord Neuberger, referring to judges, remarked in a speech to the Criminal Justice Alliance in 2015: "I dare say that we all suffer from a degree of unconscious bias". [Lord Neuberger, "Fairness in the courts: the best we can do", address to the Criminal Justice Alliance, 10 April 2015.]. The bias that Lord Neuberger appeared to be thinking of was against poor, uneducated or foreign litigants in the court. But the real bias shown by judges -- with some notable exceptions -- is very different. It is the standard "liberal" or "politically correct" bias which has recently become the dominant mindset among the "chattering classes" – favouring groups perceived as suffering discrimination, including women, minorities and the disabled, together, surprisingly enough, with special interest groups such as terror suspects, asylum seekers and even convicted killers. It would be hard to exaggerate the effect of this "unconscious bias" on the fairness of court decisions. *This topic has been dealt with in an earlier chapter.*

Privileged Killers - Venables and Thompson
One of the best examples of the privilege accorded to convicted killers is the case of Jon Venables and Robert Thompson, who brutally murdered the little James Bulger in 1993. They abducted the toddler from a shopping mall in Merseyside and then proceeded to torture and murder him. Although the killers were only 10½ years old, they were well aware of what they were doing. "One of the boys later revealed that they were planning to find a child to abduct, lead him to the busy road alongside the mall, and push him into the path of oncoming traffic." [Stephen Blease, *North-West Evening Mail*, 23 February 2009]. The killers approached James Bulger while his mother was momentarily distracted. They took him by the hand and led him on a meandering 2.5 mile hike across Liverpool, tortured him and hit him over the head with a 22-pound iron bar, fracturing his skull in ten places. So cold-blooded was this horrendous murder that the killers finally laid little Jamie's body across a railway line in the hope that it would be hit by a train, making his death appear accidental. When his body was discovered, hundreds of people laid flowers at the scene – including one of his killers, the court was told. [Jonathan Foster, *Independent*, 10 November 1993].

The Crown Court jury had no trouble finding Venables and Thompson guilty of murder. The judge condemned their crime as one of "unparalleled evil and barbarity...In my judgment, your conduct was both cunning and very wicked." The judge sentenced them to be detained at Her Majesty's pleasure (i.e. indefinitely, the standard sentence for murderers aged under 18), adding that they should be kept in custody for "very, very many years to come" – but then recommended a patently inadequate term of eight years, which was increased by the Chief Justice to a hardly more satisfactory ten years. But, so incensed was the public by the brutality of the murder and the feebleness of the judicial response that a petition bearing nearly 280,000 signatures was presented to the Home Secretary, Michael Howard, asking for the killers' sentence to be increased. Michael Howard was receptive to this clamour and announced that the killers would be kept in custody for 15 years, until they were 25 years of age.

One might have expected this to be the end of the matter, but it was far from over. In 1999, six years after the trial, lawyers representing Venables and Thompson applied to the European Court of Human Rights claiming that the killers had not had a fair trial in breach of their rights under ECHR Art 6 and that the trial amounted to inhuman and degrading treatment in breach of ECHR Art 3. The Art 3 claim was rejected, but by 16 votes to 1 the Strasbourg court upheld the claim that these murderers had been denied a fair trial: "The public trial process in an adult court must be regarded in the case of an 11-year-old child as a severely intimidating procedure." Is it really credible that these callous killers who had just committed one of the most brutal and vicious murders in the annals of British crime were shaking in their shoes at the sight of the judge's wig and red robes – hardly different from Santa Claus? Moreover, the young defendants had been given preferential treatment of a kind that is never accorded to adult defendants. The courtroom had even been specially modified to make it less intimidating to young defendants. They had had the procedure explained to them and had been given a tour of the court in advance, and the hearing times had been shortened for their convenience. One modification, a raised dock designed to give the defendants a better view, was actually fastened on as a specific cause of complaint in itself, as it was claimed that this exposed the defendants to the public gaze and made them more visible to the press. Not least, their legal representatives were seated "within whispering distance" – quite different from the usual Crown Court arrangement, where defendants are penned into a dock at the back of the court while their barristers are seated in the front. But their claim was that as a result of all the supposed indignities that they had suffered the whole situation was too tense for them to be able to participate effectively in the proceedings and they had therefore been denied a fair trial. Amazingly, these flimsy arguments carried the day in the Strasbourg court, which also accepted the argument that the Home Secretary ought not to have been involved in setting the tariff for the convicted murderers. The Strasbourg court held that the fixing of the tariff amounted to a "sentencing exercise", which formed part of the trial process and therefore infringed the killers' right under ECHR Art 6(1) to have a fair trial "by an independent and impartial tribunal established by law" – the Home Secretary being neither a tribunal nor independent of the executive, of which he was a member. [*T v. UK* 99/121 & *V v. UK* 99/122, *(Euro*pean Court of Human Rights)].

In addition to finding that the killers' Art 6 rights had been infringed, the Strasbourg court awarded them costs against the UK government, £29,000 to Venables and £15,000 to Thompson. So thoroughgoing was the murderers' victory that Jack Straw, the Home Secretary, found it necessary to comment: "This judgment does not overturn the verdict of murder, nor does it in any way exonerate the two youths for their part in this terrible crime."

With this victory under their belts, the next step was early release for the two killers, who were now 18 years old and had spent seven years in secure juvenile units, where they had enjoyed exceptionally good educational and recreational facilities. The new Chief Justice, Lord Woolf, recommended that they be released before having to be transferred to a young offenders' institution. "They are unlikely to be able to cope, at least at first, with the corrosive atmosphere with which they could be faced if transferred. There is also the danger of their being exposed to drugs." [*The Guardian*, 27 October 2000]. The idea that these two hardened killers would be likely to be "corroded" by a spell in jail -- and not even an adult prison -- would be comical if it was not so completely unrealistic. Needless to say, the Woolf "recommendation" was duly acted upon, and the two murderers were released "on life licence" (i.e. on parole) in June 2001.

But the killers' run of court successes had not yet come to an end. Their victory parade culminated in the grant to them of lifelong anonymity, which occurred just before their release in 2001. The judge, Dame Elizabeth Butler-Sloss, had no difficulty in granting them this extreme protection, citing the *Osman* case (discussed above) for the proposition that "There is a positive duty on the court as a public authority to take steps to protect individuals from the criminal acts of others" adding from the Strasbourg court's judgment in *Osman*: "The court notes that the first sentence of Article 2(1) enjoins the state not only to refrain from the intentional and unlawful taking of life, but also to take appropriate steps to safeguard the lives of those within it's *(sic)* jurisdiction." But the main basis of the judge's decision was something else: "In my judgment, this case stands or falls on the application to it of the law of confidence." [*Venables & Thompson v. News Group Newspapers* [2001] 1 All ER 908].

The grant of lifelong anonymity to Venables and Thompson rested ultimately on the perceived danger to their lives. Is it surprising that they should have received death-threats when they had apparently got away with murder? And why should the identity of these criminals be "confidential"? The whole concept of justice is that it should be open. In the oft-quoted words of Lord Chief Justice Hewart, citing a basic principle of natural law: *"It is of fundamental importance that justice should not only be done, but should manifestly and undoubtedly be seen to be done." [R v. Sussex Justices, ex parte McCarthy* [1924] 1 KB 256].

The two killers needed protection only because there was a public outcry at the perceived failure of the criminal justice system to mete out justice to the guilty. If the murderous pair had been kept in prison for 35 years -- which would not have been unreasonable in the circumstances -- or even for 15 years, the tariff set by the Home Secretary, the public hunger for justice would have been satisfied and the two killers would have been largely ignored. Taking the killers out of circulation for a good long time would not only have assuaged the public desire for condign punishment and retribution but would also have ensured that while they were sitting in prison the killers would not have posed a danger to the public.

The injunction conferring lifelong anonymity on the two murderers was and is *contra mundum* ("against the whole world"), meaning that it is enforceable not only against the named defendants in that particular case -- two major newspaper groups -- but also against "any person with notice of this order".

The injunction opens with a penal notice printed in bold capitals as stern as the curse on any Egyptian pharaoh's tomb:
"TAKE NOTICE THAT IF YOU NEGLECT TO OBEY THIS ORDER YOU MAY BE HELD IN CONTEMPT OF COURT AND LIABLE TO IMPRISONMENT OR SEQUESTRATION OF YOUR ASSETS."

So, if you divulge any information about the new identity or whereabouts of either of the murderers (including even "any description which purports to be of their physical appearance, voices or accents at any time" since their conviction in 1993), then *you* could spend time in prison – which they never did.

The real victims

In the series of court cases after their initial conviction the two killers were treated as victims. The real victims were ignored. James Bulger's right to life had been snuffed out together with his life. But his parents, Ralph and Denise, were victims too. Their grief and the strain under which their son's death placed them caused their marriage to break down. After the killers' big win in Strasbourg in March 1999, James Bulger's parents themselves applied to Strasbourg. Though granted a two-hour hearing, they were forbidden to reveal what was said in court or even what their own arguments had been! And their application was summarily rejected, presumably because they did not qualify under an unduly narrow definition of "victim". Similarly, though invited by Chief Justice Woolf to make representations after that judge's recommendation that the killers be paroled in the near future, Ralph Bulger was given short shrift by the court when he challenged the recommendation as "irrational". The court held that Ralph Bulger did not even have "a sufficient interest" or "standing" to challenge the new tariff. "The invitation extended to him to make representations as to the impact of the offence on him was not an invitation to indicate views as to the appropriate tariff": *R (on the application of Bulger) v Secretary of State* [2001] EWHC Admin 119, [2001] 3 All ER 449. Judicial review is a procedure for challenging *a decision*. What decision was Mr Bulger invited to challenge if not the decision to recommend early parole for the murderers? Ralph Bulger would not qualify as a "victim" within HRA s 7(1)(b), because the decision that he sought to challenge was not directly about himself, nor indeed even directly about his murdered little boy. However, it is important to note that he was not seeking to bring his challenge under human rights law at all but under the ordinary rules of judicial review, for which the hurdle of "sufficient interest" or "standing" is generally set very low – but not in this case.

Ian Huntley

It is perhaps worth comparing this case with another notorious murder, that of two 10-year-old girls in Soham, Cambridgeshire, by Ian Huntley in 2002. The police suspected that Huntley had killed the girls in a fit of jealous rage after a furious telephone row with his girlfriend, Maxine Carr, but the police admitted that they had found no evidence of premeditation – by contrast with Venables and Thompson, who had tried to abduct another little boy shortly before grabbing James Bulger.

Huntley was found guilty of the murder of the two girls by a majority jury verdict and was sentenced to life imprisonment, with a minimum term of 40 years, meaning that he could not be released until the age of 68. The judge commented: "The order I make offers little or no hope of the defendant's eventual release": [2005] EWHC 2083(QB), §16. This remark may have been prompted by the judge's recognition of the perilous existence of a convicted child-killer in prison – and Huntley has certainly been subjected to his fair share of attacks by fellow inmates, including an attempt on his life. Despite the clear danger to his life in prison, Huntley has never sought nor been granted special protection of any kind. And, because his sentence was certainly not too lenient but, if anything, rather too severe, there is no public rage against him.

By contrast, Huntley's girlfriend, Maxine Carr, who pleaded guilty to perverting the course of justice, was sentenced to 42 months' imprisonment and served 21 months (including 16 months on remand) *was* granted a new identity and lifelong anonymity similar to that of Venables and Thompson, Mary Bell and now "C" (see below) – on the ground that her life would otherwise be in danger. She had provided a false alibi for Huntley, claiming that she had been with him at the time of the murders when she was in fact in Grimsby. This effectively put the police off Huntley's scent for about two weeks. Once again, there apparently was a certain amount of feeling in the public mind that Maxine Carr had got off too lightly, which was heightened by her projected autobiographical book deal, which ought to have been disallowed on the basis of the much neglected legal principle that one is not allowed to profit from one's own wrongdoing but which actually came to nought only because the publisher pulled the plug in response to "scores" of public objections to the plan. [news.bbc.co.uk/1/hi/England/tyne/4310763.stm – 2 March 2005].

****

CHAPTER 9
Rights v Rights

This chapter is essentially a round-up highlighting the parlous state of human rights law in the UK at the present time – and the precarious state of your human rights as a result.

The Rule of Fairness

One of the most fundamental principles of natural justice is *audi alteram partem,* or "hear the other side". This is what is termed the rule of fairness, because the point is not only that the court should hear both sides but also that it should treat both sides fairly and not favour one against the other. Yet in human rights cases there has been a disquieting tendency to favour those claiming such rights. In a paper of 2000 kindly made available to me by Lord Steyn, that former law lord went so far as to suggest that adjudication in human rights cases "needs to be approached generously in order to afford citizens the full measure of the protections of a Bill of Rights". [See Arnheim, *Handbook of Human Rights Law,* p. 71].

There are three problems with this suggestion. First, to single out "citizens" is plainly wrong: the HRA and the ECHR apply equally to everyone in the UK, citizens and non-citizens alike. Secondly, to refer to the HRA as a "Bill of Rights" is incorrect. It is Lord Steyn's attempt to invest the HRA with the properties of a written constitution carrying higher law

Status – which it does not possess and which it is not within the power of the courts to bestow on it. Thirdly, if, as it appears, Lord Steyn's remark is intended to suggest that the person claiming human rights protection should be favoured over the person or authority against which the claim is being made, then that is blatantly unfair, both because it is a negation *of audi alteram partem* and also because it ignores the fact that there are human rights on both sides.

Two Categories

As I have stressed repeatedly in this book, every human rights case is really a case of human rights vs. human rights, even when the defendant is the government or some other public authority, because a claim against the government is really a claim against the human rights of all law-abiding members of society. Human rights cases may be divided into two broad categories in accordance with the clash of rights that they involve. The first category is made up of cases which involve competition between one person's rights under an article of the ECHR and another person's rights under the same article.

Competition over Freedom of Expression

An example of this would be the right of an invited speaker to address, say, a university student society, as against the right of opponents of that speaker to protest. In this sort of scene, which has now become commonplace particularly at universities in both the UK and the US, both the speaker and the protesters have a right to freedom of expression – unless the protest turns violent, in which case the protesters are breaking the law. But, with the ascendancy of "political correctness", the speaker too can lose the protection of the law by indulging in "hate speech", an ill-defined term which does not actually appear in any statute but which is used as a shorthand for speech criminalized in Britain by the Public Order Act 1986 and the Equality Act 2010.

Freedom of Expression vs. Privacy

This brings us to the second category of the clash of rights, namely where X's rights of one kind are in opposition to Y's rights of a different kind. The prime example is of course the clash between freedom of speech and privacy. [See Chapters 6 and 7]. For the most part this plays out in the form of competition between "celebrities" and the press. The test is supposed to be "public interest", where "public interest" does not mean the prurient interest on the part of doorstepping journalists and their readers in the private lives of "celebrities" but rather the justifiable right of the public to know. In the defamation case of *Reynolds v. Times Newspapers* [1999] 4 All ER 609 ten "matters to be taken into account" by the courts in cases of this kind were listed by Lord Nicholls, the chief one being the lamentably vague and inevitably subjective question of "the extent to which the subject-matter is a matter of public concern". Although the list contains ten "matters to be taken into account", Lord Nicolls added: "The list is not exhaustive. The weight to be given to these and any other relevant factors will vary from case to case." This qualification unfortunately only made what was already an unwieldy and vague test all the less practical. But this "Reynolds defence" was raised successfully in several subsequent defamation cases before being superseded by the statutory defence of "publication on a matter of public interest" introduced by section 4 of the Defamation Act 2013. This defence is a plus for the press because the statement in question does not have to be true – provided the defendant publisher of the statement "reasonably believed the statement complained of was in the public interest".

What is the test for the countervailing right of privacy? Unfortunately, there really isn't one, as there is no protection for privacy as such either under ECHR Article 8 or under the common law. [See Chapter 7]. As a result, as we saw in that chapter, the courts have cobbled together a law of privacy out of a gross expansion of Article 8 coupled with an extended version of the common law of confidentiality. After failing to heed the Court of Appeal's 1991 plea to protect privacy by legislation, Parliament again missed a valuable opportunity to step into the breach when it reformed the law of defamation in 2013. Privacy, after all, is the flipside of freedom of speech, which was the subject of the Defamation Act 2013. The two areas could easily have been united in a single statute, clarifying the law and preventing judges from making up the law as they went along.

Judge Bostjan Zupancic, the well-known Slovenian judge sitting on the Strasbourg court, sensibly commended as a "very good criterion" of privacy the test of a "reasonable expectation of privacy" as adumbrated by the Strasbourg court in *Halford v UK* [1997] ECHR 32 and applied in *von Hannover v. Germany (No. 1)* (2005) 40 EHRR 1 and *von Hannover v. Germany (No. 2)* (2012) 55 EHRR 15, both the latter being about photographs taken of Princess Caroline of Monaco but with somewhat different facts and opposite results.

The important case of the "Support Gay Marriage" cake, discussed in Chapter 1, is a good example of the clash of rights. The muddle in which English law finds itself in this regard is well illustrated by the case of Dale McAlpine, a Christian preacher, who was arrested and charged in 2010 under the Public Order Act 1986 for remarking to a gay Police Community Support Officer that he believed homosexual activity was contrary to the word of God. [www.telegraph.co.uk – 14 May 2010]. Although the Crown Prosecution Service dropped the charges, the preacher then sued the police for wrongful arrest, unlawful imprisonment and a violation of his human rights under ECHR Article 9 (freedom of religion) and Article 10 (freedom of expression). The police paid Dale McAlpine £7,000 (plus costs) to settle the case, together with an apology from a senior police officer. [www.newsandstar.co.uk–12 February 2010]. In a similar incident, Anthony Rollins, a Christian street preacher proclaiming that homosexuality was morally wrong and eliciting in response a shout of "homophobic bigot" was awarded £4,000 after being arrested, handcuffed and detained for three hours without even being interviewed by the police. [www.lifesitenews.com – 14 December 2010].

Favouring Claimants in Human Rights Cases

The tendency to favour human rights claimants over the defendant public authority goes back over twenty years. For example, in a case on a ban by the Ministry of Defence on employing gays, in the military, it was held both in the Divisional Court and in the Court of Appeal that, although the government's policy was not "*Wednesbury* unreasonable" (the ultimate test in judicial review) the proper approach in cases challenging government administrative decisions was as follows:

"The court may not interfere with the exercise of an administrative discretion on substantive grounds save where the court is satisfied that the decision is unreasonable in the sense that it is beyond the range of responses open to a reasonable decision-maker. But in judging whether the decision-maker has exceeded this margin of appreciation the human rights context is important. The more substantial the interference with human rights, the more the court will require by way of justification before it is satisfied that the decision is reasonable in the sense outlined above." [*R (Smith) v. Secretary of State for Defence* [1995] EWCA Civ 22].

There are two problems here: first, taking it for granted that there has been some interference with the claimant's rights;

and secondly, having a sliding scale of "unreasonableness", which again favours the claimant. The result is simply unfair and wrong.

Curiously enough, the "applicable test" adopted both in the Divisional Court and in the Court of Appeal was one suggested by counsel for the gay service personnel, yet the outcome of this case in the UK domestic courts upheld government policy. In Strasbourg the Government lost, on the ground that its policy violated the gay service members' rights under ECHR Article 8: "Everyone has the right to respect for his private.....life...." [*Smith & Grady v. UK* (1999) 29 EHRR 493]. Scant attention was paid to the rights of heterosexual service members which might be impacted by this ruling. Another case where the fact that the case was one of rights vs. rights was lost sight of – not to mention the "margin of appreciation" (or "margin of state discretion") that should have been left to the UK Government, an important principle allowing individual member states (generally wide) scope "to derogate from the obligations laid down in the Convention".

As for the test adopted by the courts from the barrister representing one of the parties in the case, that in itself is worrying. For one thing, counsel represents one side in a dispute. How surprising would it be if that test was not entirely neutral? Moreover, why do the judges have to rely on a test proposed by counsel? Do they not have their own test – a proper neutral test? This only underlines the terrible muddle besetting English law – and, unfortunately, not only in the area of public law.

Lord Irvine, a former Lord Chancellor, and a constant repository of sound common sense, commented: "The approach adopted in *Brind*, which states conclusively that the *Wednesbury* threshold of unreasonableness is not lowered in fundamental rights cases, must prevail." [Lord Irvine, "Judges and decision-makers: the theory and practice of Wednesbury review", *Public Law*, vol. 59 (1996) at 65].

"The Oxygen of Publicity"

Brind was an interesting case involving national security. In 1988 Prime Minister Margaret Thatcher issued notices to the BBC and the Independent Broadcasting Authority requiring them "to refrain at all times from sending any broadcast matter.....where the person speaking the words represents or purports to represent" certain named organizations. This was done in order to starve these organizations of what Mrs Thatcher called "the oxygen of publicity". The broadcasting media easily got round this over-precise wording by having the offending words dubbed by a "voice over". This resulted in the comical spectacle of spokespeople for the named organizations being seen on television but appearing to speak in a mellifluous actor's voice instead of in their own sometimes less than perfectly modulated tones. So, far from starving them of the oxygen of publicity, the government order gave them greater publicity than ever, plus novel entertainment value.

One may wonder, then, why a legal challenge was mounted against the government's directives. In fact, the case, brought by a number of broadcast journalists, went all the way up to the House of Lords: *Brind v. Secretary of State for the Home Department* [1991] 1 All ER 720. The government sought to justify its directives on the ground that they were necessary in the public interest to combat terrorism. In the judicial review hearings in the English domestic courts it was held that this reasoning could hardly be regarded as "Wednesbury unreasonable". In the words of Lord Ackner: "It would be a wrongful usurpation of power by the judiciary to substitute its, the judicial view, on the merits and on that basis to quash the decision." And even the Strasbourg Commission of Human Rights found no violation of ECHR Article 10. Strasbourg recognized "the need to protect the State and the public against armed conspiracies seeking to overthrow the democratic order which guarantees this freedom and other human rights.". The UK's measures were found to be "not disproportionate to the aim sought to be pursued" and "bearing in mind the margin of appreciation permitted to States", the Strasbourg Commission found in favour of the UK Government. [*Brind v. UK*, Admissibility Application 18714/91].

The term "Wednesbury unreasonableness" comes from the leading case about judicial review, in which Lord Greene MR identified the two chief criteria for striking down a government administrative decision as (a) illegality and (b) acting *ultra vires*, or exceeding its powers. If neither of these tests was satisfied the decision in question would be legal and all "within the four corners of the law" – unless it was "so unreasonable that no reasonable authority could ever have come to it". This exception, which was not found to exist in the Wednesbury case itself, was so extreme as to be a near-impossibility. But it has been whittled down over the years so as to make it easier to find liability. [*Associated Provincial Picture Houses v. Wednesbury* [1948] 1 KB 223].

Lord Irvine of Lairg (Lord Chancellor 1997-2003) remarked: "The approach adopted in *Brind*, which states conclusively that the Wednesbury threshold of unreasonableness is not lowered in fundamental rights cases, must prevail." [Lord Irvine, "Judges and Decision-makers", (1996) *Public Law* 59 at 65]. This salutary warning has, alas, not been heeded. Instead the courts have tended to move towards a "merits review" of administrative decisions, which is in danger of substituting the court's decision for that of the original decision-maker – something that is supposed to be a complete no-no as far as judicial review is concerned. [See M. Arnheim, *Handbook of Human Rights Law*, p44ff.].

Equality Act Trumps Employment Law

The effect of the Equality Act 2010 even on an otherwise apparently straightforward employment matter is well illustrated by the following case: *Southwark London BC v. Charles* UKEAT/0008/14/RN – 22 July 2014. The Claimant, Mr Charles, was made redundant when his own job disappeared. He was eligible for redeployment and was required to attend a formal interview for the position of Noise Support Officer, for which he was one of ten candidates. However, because of his disability the Claimant was unable "to attend administrative meetings including redeployment interviews". Southwark Council was held by an Employment Tribunal to have discriminated against him by failing to make "reasonable adjustments", which would have dispensed with the need for such an interview. The Council was therefore held to be in breach of its duties to the Claimant under both section 15 and section 20 of the Equality Act 2010. This decision was upheld by appeal to the Employment Appeal Tribunal.

In more detail: The Claimant, Mr Charles, was found by an Employment Tribunal to have been fairly dismissed for redundancy resulting from a re-organization leading to the "deletion" of his grade 9 post as an Environmental Enforcement Officer with the Council. Two months prior to this the Claimant had been "suspended from work for allegedly falsifying documents". But at a disciplinary meeting the Claimant "produced a letter from his general practitioner explaining that his health problems could have caused what was described as this 'procedural error'." Yet the Claimant won his case against the Council. In the words of the single judge sitting in the Employment Appeal Tribunal: The Employment Tribunal found that the Claimant's dismissal "was by reason of redundancy and that the procedure was fair. Nevertheless it found that the Claimant, to the knowledge of the Respondent, suffered from a disability, an inability to attend administrative meetings including redeployment interviews, and that the Respondent had both discriminated against him by requiring him to attend such an interview and had failed to make reasonable adjustments by dispensing with the need for such an interview and that in consequence he was placed at a substantial disadvantage by being dismissed. The Employment Tribunal therefore found that the Respondent was in breach of its duties, both under section 15 and under section 20 of the Equality Act 2010." Section 15 of the Equality Act 2010 prohibits "discrimination arising from disability" and section 20 is about the duty to make "reasonable adjustments" for a disabled person.

This case is far from unique, which is all the more disquieting. It highlights several serious problems with human rights law in the UK today:

a) Both the Employment Tribunal and the Employment Appeal Tribunal appear to have focused exclusively on the rights of the Claimant, who was one of ten candidates for the post of Noise Support Officer.

b) After being suspended for allegedly falsifying documents, the Claimant "produced a letter from his general practitioner explaining that his health problems could have caused what was described as this 'procedural error'." Falsifying documents is a potentially serious allegation. No independent medical evidence was called to substantiate the GP's explanation that it "could" have been caused by the Claimant's health problems.

c) And what exactly was his disability? His condition is described in the judgment as "sleep paralysis agitans and depression". The EAT report added that the Claimant's counsel "has helpfully explained that that was a condition in which the Claimant woke up at night, paralysed. And so felt unable to go back to sleep. Unsurprisingly, that led to the depression which the general practitioner diagnosed." In *Fitzgerald's Clinical Neuroanatomy and Neuroscience* (2015), a standard medical practitioner's text on the subject, "paralysis agitans" is described as "an archaic term. See *Parkinson's disease.*" It refers to the "shaking palsy" or tremor characteristic of Parkinson's disease, but, contrary to the description given to the Tribunal by counsel, it is not "paralysis" in the normal sense of that word. The full term, "sleep paralysis agitans", is not a recognized disease. Sleep disturbance is often associated with Parkinson's disease, but it is described very differently from the way it was described to the Tribunal. In a 2014 article in the Journal of Neural Transmission, Dr William Ondo of the University of Texas Health Science Center wrote: "More recent studies have confirmed that the majority of patients with Parkinson's disease (PD) suffer from some sleep disturbances. This can manifest as falling or staying asleep, fractionated sleep, specific parasomnias, and daytime sleepiness." ["Sleep/wake problems in Parkinson's disease: pathophysiology and clinicopathologic correlations", *Journal of Neural Transmission* (Vienna) 2014 Aug [www.ncbi.nim.nih.gov.pubmed/24858728]. This raises a number of questions: (i) The only evidence of the Claimant's condition is from counsel's "explanation" of a GP's diagnosis. The GP does not appear to have given evidence to the Employment Tribunal. (ii) Why was expert medical evidence not called? (iii) If the diagnosis was essentially one of Parkinson's disease, why is that not mentioned? (iv) And was the Claimant on medication for his condition? Because there are some very effective medications available for Parkinson's.

d) Even if the diagnosis and the description of the symptoms passed muster after proper evidence and cross-examination, there would still need to have been proper proof of the causation linking the Claimant's condition to his inability to attend "administrative meetings" as well as redeployment interviews. There was also apparently no questioning of his suitability for deployment at all if he was unable even to attend "administrative meetings", which most public sector posts would require.

e) The decision effectively required the Claimant to be accorded *special privileges* as against the others with whom he was competing for redeployment. Is that really what the Equality Act is intended to do?

Common Law Rights vs. ECHR Rights

As if there were not already enough worrying manifestations of judicial activism, there has been a recent tendency on the part of a few senior judges to invoke principles supposedly enshrined in the common law as having at least equal authority with the (already bloated and expanded) Convention rights. An example of this occurred in a 2004 case involving the admission of evidence allegedly obtained by torture. Both the Special Immigration Appeals Commission (SIAC) and the Court of Appeal decided that, though the common law prohibits torture, unless it could be shown that the evidence in question had been "obtained by torture which the State (i.e. the UK) has procured or connived at", there was no basis for excluding it. But this decision was reversed by a 4:3 majority in the House of Lords, which was the highest court at the time.

Lord Justice Laws in the Court of Appeal held as follows: "[T]he constitutional principle which forbids abuse of State power rules out reliance by the Secretary of State, before SIAC or any other tribunal in this jurisdiction, upon any statement obtained by torture which the State has procured or connived at. But I am quite unable to see that any such principle prohibits the Secretary of State from relying....on evidence coming into his hands which has or may have been obtained through torture by agencies of other States over which he has no power of direction. If he has neither procured the torture nor connived at it, he has not offended the constitutional principle which I have sought to outline. In that case the focus shifts, as it seems to me, back to the law of evidence. Given that the specific rule against involuntary confessions is not engaged (we are not dealing with tortured defendants), the general rule – evidence is admissible if it is relevant, and the court is not generally concerned with its provenance –

applies....Any other approach seems to me to be replete with difficulty. First, I cannot believe that the law should sensibly impose on the Secretary of State a duty of solemn enquiry as to the interrogation methods used by agencies of other sovereign States. Apart from the practical unreality, I can find no sound juridical base for the imposition of such a requirement." [Laws LJ in *A et al, Mahmoud Abu Rideh, Jamal Ajouaou v. Secretary of State for the Home Department* [2004] EWCA Civ 1123, §252ff.].

Towards the end of his eminently sensible judgment, Laws LJ dismissed a supplementary submission made on behalf of (some of) the applicants, namely that admission of the evidence in question would be contrary to Article 15 of the United Nations Convention against Torture (CAT). Laws LJ rejected this argument out of hand: "If it were viable at all, it would require the demonstration of actual violations of Article 15 by the UK. None are demonstrated...This argument is, I fear, nothing but an attempt to municipalise our obligations under CAT Article 15 and that is something that only the legislature can do." Article 15 of CAT provides: "Each State Party that any statement which is established to have been made as a result of torture shall not be invoked as evidence in any proceedings, except against a person accused of torture as evidence that the statement was made." So, even according to this there has to be proof that the evidence in question was procured by torture.

Laws LJ added a postscript to his beautifully logical and responsible judgment to dispatch the applicants "submission to the effect that CAT Article 15 expressed a principle of international customary law, and as such was part of the fabric of the common law. That would have required a very substantial enquiry, legal and historical. The ground has not been prepared for it" and counsel was not permitted to embark upon it.

Despite the rejection by SIAC and the Court of Appeal of the application for exclusion of *possibly* torture-procured evidence (of which there was no proof), the House of Lords reversed those decisions and decided, partly on the basis of a supposed principle of common law, evidence should not be admitted if it was alleged that "it may have been procured by torture. The contrary approach would place on the detainee a burden of proof which, for reasons beyond his control, he can seldom discharge. In practice that would largely nullify the principle, vigorously supported on all sides, that courts will not admit evidence procured by torture. That would be to pay lip-service to the principle. That is not good enough." [Lord Nicholls in: *A (FC) and others v. Secretary of State for the Home Department* [2005] UKHL 71, §80]. What principle is that? The actual common law principle, as stated by Laws LJ in the Court of Appeal, is that relevant evidence can be excluded only if it was "obtained by torture which the State (i.e. the UK) has procured or connived at" - but a bare assertion without any proof of the allegation cannot be taken seriously. Any barrister who has had any involvement with this area of the law will know just how easy it is to make these vague allegations. Moreover, the common law has no applicability to what happens in foreign countries.

Three of the seven law lords did at least disagree with the majority in an important respect. Here is Lord Rodger's dissent: "My noble and learned friend, Lord Bingham of Cornhill (for the majority) proposes....that the statement should be excluded whenever SIAC is unable to conclude that there is not a real risk that the evidence has been obtained by torture. It respectfully appears to me that this would be to replace the true rule, that statements obtained by torture must be excluded, with a significantly different rule, that statements must be excluded unless there is not a real risk that they have been obtained by torture. In effect, the true rule would be inverted. There is no warrant for Lord Bingham's preferred rule in the common law, in Article 15 of CAT or elsewhere in international law....It would mean that exclusion would be liable to become the rule rather than the exception. It would encourage objections. It would prevent SIAC from relying on statements which were in fact obtained quite properly." Ibid, §145].

All this to-ing and fro-ing was in danger of turning national security into a parlour game. One thing that this kind of dissonant argumentation does *not* do is to establish the common law as an overriding basis for deciding human rights cases – because it muddies the water about what the common law principles actually are. This is exactly the opposite of the assertion made by Lord Reed, who is probably now the main protagonist of this approach: "[W]hen the House of Lords rejected the admission of evidence obtained by torture in *A v. Secretary of State for the Home Department*, it did so on the basis of the common law: Lord Bingham observed that English common law had regarded torture and its fruits with abhorrence for over 500 years, and concluded that the principles of the common law, standing alone, compelled the exclusion of third party torture evidence. He noted that that was consistent with the Convention. [Lord Reed, "The Common Law and the ECHR", Inner Temple, 11 November 2013].

As we saw above, the "abhorrence" of the common law for torture is not a sufficient basis for the House of Lords decision, because the true common law principle is the one expressed by Laws LJ in the Court of Appeal – namely that all relevant evidence is admissible unless "obtained by torture which the State (i.e. the UK) has procured or connived at": the common law is not concerned with the compilation of evidence in foreign jurisdictions.

Lord Reed has arguably fallen into the same error himself in applying supposed common law principles in other cases. In *R (Osborn) v. Parole Board* [2013] UKSC 61, he sought to redefine the relationship between the ECHR and the common law: "The guarantees set out in the substantive articles of the Convention....are mostly expressed at a very high level of generality. They have to be fulfilled at national level through a substantial body of much more specific domestic law.....The Convention taken by itself is too inspecific *[sic]* to provide the guidance which is necessary in a state governed by the rule of law....The Convention cannot therefore be treated as if it were Moses and the Prophets. On the contrary, the European court has often referred to 'the fundamentally subsidiary role of the Convention' (see eg Hatton v. UK (2003) 37 EHRR 28 § 97)." Accordingly, according to Lord Reed, recourse must be had to the common law. In *Osborn*, which concerned the treatment of prisoners, this meant "the common law standards of procedural fairness". The main problem with this approach is that there is no agreed definition of these standards, which gives the judges the power to make law, which of course encroaches on the preserve of Parliament notwithstanding Parliament's general disinclination to control the common law by legislation, which it is not only fully entitled but also obliged to do. Parliament's dereliction of duty in this regard has resulted in the common but erroneous belief that the judges are entitled to keep changing the common law. Here is a typical statement of that erroneous belief:

"Reforming the common law by statute is not an easy task (...). One of the difficulties is that the common law is constantly developing. The state of the law when the reforms are originally proposed may be different from the state of the law if and when they are eventually enacted. Indeed, the law may continue to move on even after the reforms have been enacted. The law reformer will rarely wish to preclude such organic development unless (unlike the 1977 Act) the reform is intended to be a complete codification." Torts (Interference with Goods) Act 1977." [OBG v. Allan [2007] UKHL 21, §315, *per* Baroness Hale].

Lord Buckmaster's statement of the position of the Common Law made in his dissenting speech in *Donoghue v. Stevenson* [1932] UKHL 100 still remains correct: "The law applicable is the common law, and, though its principles are capable of application to meet new conditions not contemplated when the law was laid down, these principles cannot be changed nor can additions be made to them because any particular meritorious case seems outside their ambit." Lord Buckmaster was looking at the common law from the point of view of the judiciary, and what he is saying is that judges cannot change or even add to the principles of the common law. Parliament of course can do that, in keeping with the Sovereignty of Parliament, the bedrock principle of the British constitution.

The Right to Strike

Another important right which clashes with other rights is the right to strike. When this right comes to court it is generally the rights of the strikers that are focused on, not the rights of the public, which is most likely to be harmed by the strike.

At the time of writing strikes appear to be increasing in number and intensity again, although still well below their heyday in pre-Thatcher Britain. The 1959 comedy film, "I'm All Right Jack" satirized the selfish attitudes and ulterior motives of those on both sides of the picket line, but particularly of politically motivated trade union officials. The title of the film is a contraction of the popular phrase, "F.... you, Jack. I'm all right", epitomizing the smug complacent selfish attitude of striking workers. Unlike the setting of that movie, a privately owned factory, most strikes at the present time take place among public or pseudo-public employees. The right to strike originated as part of collective bargaining between employer and employees. Withdrawing one's labour is the ultimate weapon of a worker against his employer. Doing so is a breach of contract, entitling the employer to sack the striking employees. As employers did not want to see their businesses suffer and workers did not want to lose their jobs, it was usually possible to reach an amicable settlement. When the miners went on strike in 1926, King George V rounded on the mine-owners, remarking, "Try living on their wages before you judge them." But the present situation is quite different. For one thing, the strikers of today are generally far from impoverished. Railway workers, for example, are extremely well paid, and even the so-called junior doctors are hardly on the breadline.

Secondly, strikes generally no longer affect the employers but the public, so there is less of an incentive on the employers' part to settle, and the public, who bear the brunt of the strikes, have no say.

In typical British fashion, the situation has lurched from one crisis to another. The serious and long-running dispute of GTR with ASLEF, the train-drivers' union, crippled Southern Rail services in 2016-17 causing "substantial inconvenience to many thousands of commuters", as the Court of Appeal put it. ASLEF was objecting to the extension of driver-only operation to all Southern trains, which the first-instance judge in the High Court said was "perfectly safe both in Southern and elsewhere in the UK."[www.theguardian.com – 8 December 2016]. Yet the employers lost both in the High Court and in the Court of Appeal. [*Govia GTR Railway Ltd v. ASLEF* [2016] EWCA Civ 1309]. The employers' argument was largely based on EU law, which on the one hand recognizes the right to strike as a fundamental right but does so subject to certain important restrictions. One authority relied upon by the employers was *Laval un Partneri Ltd v. Svenska Byggnadsarbetareförbundet* C-341/05 [2008] IRLR 171, a case about the freedom to provide cross-border services, in which the European Court of Justice (ECJ) found the Swedish trade union's industrial action "an unlawful interference" with the employer's right to provide cross-border services within the EU, which would therefore "frustrate the purposes of creating a free market." The relevance to the ASLEF case was that ASLEF's industrial action had a major impact on rail services into Gatwick Airport, an international airport served on two different routes by a single rail operator providing 96% of all rail services into Gatwick. However the English Court of Appeal refused to apply the *Laval* case to this situation. The court stressed that in *Laval* "it was the deterrent effect of the object of the strike, rather than the effect of the strike itself considered independently of that object, which constituted the unlawful restriction on the provision of services…..In our judgment, it is absolutely plain for the reason we have given that it is the object or purpose of the industrial action and not the damage caused by the action itself which renders it potentially subject to the freedom of movement provisions." But what proof is there of the purpose of the ASLEF strike? The employers informed the court that "Even if all safety concerns were satisfied, they [ASLEF] have indicated that they would still take industrial action." If this was true it would indicate that the purpose of the ASLEF strike was not only about driver-only operation but was essentially political – and, as the Court of Appeal recognized, "strikes with a political objective are not protected in law". However, the underlying political purpose of the strike was not pleaded by the employer, and so the Court of Appeal did not take that possibility into account. That is a weakness in the way the employer's case was handled. But the ultimate decision of the Court of Appeal is also less than persuasive. Its insistence that it was only the object or purpose of the strike that was relevant to its lawfulness, not the effect of the strike itself is by no means certain. Where does that supposed rule come from? The Court makes a worrying remark in this connection: "Furthermore, were the strike itself to be the relevant restriction, this would have profound effects on the legality of strike action." [§43]. The court here at least admits the possibility that it is the strike itself, and not just its purpose, that is relevant to its lawfulness.

This remark is disquieting, as the court seems concerned that this might result in strike action being often found to be unlawful. Why should that be a problem? I for one, together with the general public who would prefer not to be at the mercy of greedy railway workers, would welcome that. The

ECJ recognizes the fundamental right to strike, but in a number of cases has found strikes to be unlawful. Why can't the UK courts do the same?

It remains to be seen how the UK Supreme Court disposes of this important case.

"Junior Doctors'" Strike

Probably the most troubling of all recent strikes is the series of "junior doctors'" strikes in 2016. My blog on this appeared in the *Huffington Post* on 6 September 2016, when, while claiming to want to "protect" or "save" the NHS, the junior doctors were putting patients' lives at risk by threatening a series of four 5-day strikes starting on 12-16 September. 2016. These 20 days of strikes would have entailed "full withdrawal of labour" between 8:00 am and 5:00 pm on the days concerned and would have affected Accident & Emergency as well as other departments. Chris Hopson, head of NHS Providers, estimated that this would have resulted in the cancellation of over 500,000 operations plus four million outpatient appointments. [*ITV News*, 2 September 2016].

It had been reported that "junior doctors being hired to co-ordinate strike action are being paid up to £250-a-day....as well as expenses for hotels and business-class travel." [*The Sun*, 3 September 2016, report by Amanda Devlin].

This latest threat came in the wake of five strikes in January, February, March and April 2016, which resulted in the cancellation of 150,000 operations and outpatient appointments.

Strike Ballots – the Law

In law, any strike action is automatically a breach of contract. To save a strike from being unlawful -- and therefore entitling the employer to sack the strikers -- a strike ballot has to be held. But, a valid ballot must follow certain precise rules, the whole point being to prevent strikes which do not have the support of the majority of the employees concerned.

The rules governing strike ballots are laid down by the Trade Union and Labour Relations (Consolidation) Act 1992 ("TULRA"). The only valid strike ballot in the whole of the junior doctors' dispute was held on 19 November 2015, long before there was any suggestion of 5-day all-out strikes.

TULRA s.234(1) stipulates that a strike ballot "ceases to be effective" a maximum of eight weeks after the date of the ballot. So, the strike action must start within that time. S.233(3)(a) makes it clear that a ballot is needed not only for a trade union to call for its members to strike initially but also to "continue to take part in industrial action". In other words, a fresh ballot is needed for the continuation of a strike. Not only must the employer be notified of any strike ballot, but the notice must state "whether industrial action is intended to be continuous or discontinuous and specifies" the intended dates. [TULRA s. 234A(3)(b)].

Background -- Rejected Contract

On 18 May 2016, after ten days of intensive talks, it was announced that a new contract had been agreed between the BMA and the Government. Johann Malawana, the then junior doctors' leader, described this as "a good deal for junior doctors". Under the agreed contract, all juniors would get a basic pay rise of about 10%, plus a further 10% boost for those regularly working at weekends, plus an extra 37% (down from the current rate of 50%) for weekday nightshift working. However, the junior doctors proceeded to reject the agreed contract. But, as Health Secretary Jeremy Hunt pointed out: "The BMA's figures show that only 40% of those eligible actually voted against this contract, and a third of BMA members didn't vote at all." [*The Guardian*, 5 July 2016].

Secret Ballot – Only 31.5% in Favour of New Strikes

After the agreed-and-then-rejected new contract, the BMA, the doctors' trade union, seems to have recognised the need for a fresh ballot for the series of full – on strikes starting on 12 September. They did in fact hold a fresh ballot in August 2016 – but, contrary to TULRA, they kept it secret. It is perhaps not surprising that they chose to keep it from the Government, because the support for full-on strikes was nowhere near the 50% requirement for a lawful strike.

According to documents leaked to the *Daily Mail*, of the 37,770 junior doctors who as members of the BMA were entitled to vote, only 7,540, or 20%, actually voted, and of those just 31.5% (2,375) voted for the new strikes. <u>In other words, the threatened new strikes have the support of only **6.3%** of the total number of junior doctors entitled to vote</u>. [*Daily Mail*, 4 September 2016, reported by Amie Gordon, Sophie Borland & Vanessa Allen].

Despite the ballot result, the BMA council nevertheless authorised a five-day strike by junior doctors starting on 12 September 2016. When interviewed by Nick Robinson, BMA Chairman Mark Porter repeatedly refused to give details of this council vote but failed to deny that it was as close as 16 votes to 14. [*Huffington Post*, 1 September 2016, report by Aubrey Allegretti; *Daily Telegraph* 1 September 2016, report by Henry Bodkin].

The legal position on 6 September 2016 therefore was that the threatened new round of strikes was unlawful and the strikers could be sacked by their employer, the British Government. Whether influenced by my blog or not, on 24 September 2016 the junior doctors announced that they were suspending the threatened strikes "following concerns over patient safety"! And on 28 September 2016 the group "Justice for Health" mounted a legal challenge to the Government claiming that the contract was "unsafe and unsustainable" and that the Government did not have the right to impose it. Mr Justice Green ruled that Health Secretary Jeremy Hunt had acted "squarely" within his powers by calling for the NHS trusts to introduce the new contract without forcing it on anyone. The trusts, the judge held, had the freedom to decide whether or not they wanted to force the contract on doctors. The judge concluded: "On no basis can it be said that the position taken by the Minister was irrational or lacking a proper evidential basis." [*R (Justice for Health Ltd) v. Secretary of State for Health* [2016] EWHC 2338 (Admin)].

This was an extremely gratifying outcome not only for the Government but also for the thousands of people who depend on the NHS every day. But it does not actually solve the strike problem. These two alternative courses of action were open to Jeremy Hunt on 6 September 2016, and will still be open to him if the strikes start again:

- **To threaten to fire all the strikers.** In order to be lawful, any new strike action needs to be supported by over 50% of those voting in a fresh strike ballot. In the secret strike ballot held in August 2016 there was insufficient support for strike action: 31.5% is a far cry from 50%. Participants in an unlawful strike can be dismissed. The Government will be afraid to take this step in case it depletes the NHS of junior medical staff. In reality, most junior doctors threatened with dismissal if they fail to report for duty by a given date will probably see sense, remember their obligations to the public under the Hippocratic oath, and go back to work. In any case, are striking medics really indispensable to the NHS who are prepared to play politics with public health and safety? There is no shortage of foreign doctors who would be only too happy to step into the breach.
- **To activate the Trade Union Act 2016.** Amazingly, this relevant law that received the royal assent on 4 May 2016 has not yet been brought into effect! This Act requires a valid strike ballot to have not only the support of over 50% of those voting but also a turnout

of at least 50% of those entitled to vote. In (as yet undefined) "important public services", which must surely include the NHS, there is an additional requirement "that at least 40% of those who were entitled to vote in the ballot answered 'Yes' to the question." The Government originally proposed to include a provision allowing employers to hire agency workers to cover for striking employees. This important provision was dropped, but it urgently needs to be inserted for public sector strikes. This would have to be passed through Parliament as an emergency with retrospective effect, which, though exceptional, is perfectly legal.

Strikes are starting to cripple Britain again. They damage ordinary law-abiding people going about their daily business. As this book was going to press it was announced (on 16 February 2017) that Southern Rail drivers had just rejected (by 54% to 46%) the compromise deal agreed with their employer *by their own trade union, Aslef.* The other rail union, RMT, had already condemned this deal as a "shocking betrayal" of workers and passengers. [Independent 4 February 2017]. As a result, the strike will continue to cripple Southern England, including all those traveling to Gatwick Airport. And what is the strike about? It's in opposition to driver-only trains, which have run successfully in many countries around the world, including Japan, Denmark, New Zealand – and even Britain, where Driver Only Operation

(DOO) is already in use in about 30% of all mainline passenger services, the London Underground and the Docklands Light Railway. In a report published on 21 June 2016, the Rail Safety and Standards Board (RSSB), an independent body charged with assisting the rail industry to improve safety, stated: "No increased risk from properly implemented Driver Only Operation has been detected in any research carried out by RSSB or its predecessor organisation 'Rail Safety'."—[www.rssb.co.uk]. The problem will not be solved until or unless the government grasps the nettle and passes a law through Parliament outlawing strikes by public workers – as has been the case in the United States since 1947. This will not be easy to achieve in Britain, for at least three reasons, but until it is done, you, the law-abiding hard-working majority of the population will continue to be made fun of by arrogant greedy groups who care nothing about you. The three problems are:

a) The ban on strikes must cover all those whose strike is likely to harm the public. At present railway workers, for example, are not technically public employees, but they must obviously be included in the strike ban.

b) The UK government lacks the guts to confront this problem;

c) Even if they plucked up the courage to do something, the courts are quite likely to become intransigent.

In 1981 US President Ronald Reagan was confronted with a strike of air traffic controllers called by their trade union, known as the Professional Air Traffic Controllers

Organization (PATCO). They were striking for better pay, a 32-hour work week and other benefits. As employees of the federal government air traffic controllers were not allowed to strike under the Taft-Hartley Act of 1947. President Reagan took the bull by the horns and announced: "They are in violation of the law and if they do not report for work within 48 hours they have forfeited their jobs and will be terminated." Only 1,300 of the nearly 13,000 strikers returned to work. The remaining 11,345 who had ignored the order were fired and were banned from federal service for life (although this ban was lifted by President Bill Clinton in 1993). The President's action did not result in an increase in accidents in the air. Transportation Secretary Drew Lewis organized replacements and started contingency plans. The PATCO union was decertified and ceased to exist. Reagan's decisive action in the face of a potentially ruinous strike, in the words of Richard Sharpe, "lay down a marker for his presidency".

In the UK the police and prison officers are already banned from taking strike action, under the Criminal Justice and Public Order Act 1994. But in November 2016 a number of prison officers held "protest meetings" which the Prison Officers' Association (POA) claimed was not a strike. Also, the wording of the ban on strikes is inept, as what it bans is not striking as such but "inducing" a prison officer to strike. Nevertheless, on 15 November 2016 the Government was granted an injunction ordering about 10,000 prison officers to return to work.

Chapter 10
Q&A – A Socratic Dialogue

Privacy

Q. Is there a right of privacy in the UK?

A. Not really. ECHR Article 8 covers "respect for private life" but not privacy. And there is a common law of confidentiality. Both of these have been extended by the courts, especially the UK domestic courts, to cover privacy. But the result is far from satisfactory, because there are no agreed criteria, and in any event, it is highly artificial to suggest that an invasion of privacy has resulted from a breach of confidence, when the two parties may not have had any prior contact with each other. [See Chapters 5 & 6].

Q. Isn't privacy also protected by the Data Protection Act 1998?

A. Supposedly. But the rules are so complicated that they are quite often used not so much to protect genuine privacy interests as to enable some organizations to hide behind it and refuse to disclose information which is really in the public domain.

Q. So what then is the function of the Freedom of Information Act 2000?

A. That is supposed to create a public "right of access" to information held by public authorities, but it has also been the subject of some surprising decisions.

Q. Such as?
A. Such as the case about the request made by a journalist for access to private letters from Prince Charles to government ministers. The Attorney General declined the request as being an invasion of privacy, but the UK Supreme Court by a majority of 5:2 allowed publication of the letters. [*R (Evans} v. Attorney General* [2015] UKSC 21].
Q. Do you think that decision was correct?
A. No, I think the two hard-hitting dissenting opinions were right. They both made the point that the majority had exceeded their powers. Lord Hughes (who dissented on the main issue) stressed that "the rule of law is not the same as a rule that courts must always prevail, no matter what the statute says." In his dissent Lord Wilson said that "the majority did not in my view interpret section 53 of the Freedom of Information Act. It rewrote it. It invoked precious constitutional principles, but among the most precious is that of parliamentary sovereignty, emblematic of our democracy." What Lord Wilson was saying was therefore that the majority decision amounted to a usurpation of parliamentary power – a serious constitutional issue.

Privacy vs. Press Freedom
Q. Why has Parliament not passed a law protecting privacy, as has occurred in a number of other countries?
A. After the case of *Gorden Kaye v. Robertson* [1991] FSR 62, Lord Justice Glidewell in the Court of Appeal implored Parliament to step into the breach. In 1993 the Calcutt

Report also recommended the introduction of a law of privacy. But, because of media opposition, nothing was ever done.

Q. The press always stress the importance to democracy of a free press. But how does that affect your freedom of expression as a law-abiding individual?

A. The press are of course very concerned to uphold their freedom to report whatever they consider to be in the "public interest", but what that really means is to intrude into the private life of individuals like yourself.

Q. But the press are big supporters of everybody's freedom of speech, aren't they?

A. That's the impression that they like to create, but they aren't really interested in *your* freedom of speech.

Q. Really?

A. Well, just try to get a newspaper to apologize to you or to retract some false statement that they made about you! Or to be heard in their columns or on radio or TV.

Q. You mean they keep a tight control over who says what in their columns and airwaves?

A. Precisely. But they want to be given as much latitude as possible. The "phone hacking scandal" revealed in 2011 led to no more than seven convictions. This was followed by the Leveson Inquiry of 2011-12, which found that press regulation by the Press Complaints Commission (PCC) was ineffectual and recommended a new system, which stopped well short of statutory regulation of the press, which is badly needed. What emerged was a new and again entirely voluntary regulator called the Independent Press Standards Organisation (IPSO), which was soon condemned as being just as ineffectual as the PCC and just as much under the control of the media which it was supposed to regulate.

Q. Don't we have more to fear from government "snooping" than from an intrusive press?

A. There's a lot of hype about the so-called "Snooper's Charter". In fact, what government security agencies collect is not data but *metadata*, or "information that provides information about other data". It has been likened to an itemized phone bill, which does not identify any names, bank account numbers or even email addresses – and certainly not any of the content of the listed phone-calls. For that special permission has to be obtained.

Q. But Wikileaks' Julian Assange as well as Edward Snowden and Chelsea (previously Bradley) Manning claim to have done us a service by hacking into (primarily US) government computer records and disclosing them.

A. What is really worrying is the ease with which all these government records were hacked, potentially endangering not only government anti-terrorist programs but also thousands of lives. In 2013 Manning was sentenced by a US court martial to 35 years' imprisonment after pleading guilty to 10 out of a total of 22 charges. She apologized to the court: "I am sorry that my actions hurt people. I'm sorry that they hurt the United States. I am sorry for the unintended consequences of my actions. When I made these decisions I believed I was going to help people, not hurt people." ["Chelsea Manning" – Wikipedia].

Q. But Chelsea Manning was pardoned by outgoing President Obama, wasn't she?

A. In January 2017 her sentence was commuted to serving only another four months, as being "disproportionate relative to what other leakers have obtained". President Obama added: "It makes sense to commute – and not pardon – her sentence." [CBS News, 17 January 2017]. Not surprisingly, President Trump remarked that Manning should "never have been released". [Fox News, 26 January 2017].

Q. But all these leaks have also been highly praised in certain quarters, haven't they?

A. Needless to say. But in 2010 Assange was asked by Amnesty International and other human rights groups to "redact" (i.e. edit out) from their disclosed files the names of Afghan civilians working as US military informants, in order to protect these people from repercussions. When Amnesty International "appeared to express reservations" in accepting Assange's offer of the opportunity to assist in the tedious document vetting process, Assange remarked that he had "no time to deal with people who prefer to do nothing but cover their asses". [Jeanne Whalen, "Human Rights Groups Press Wikileaks Over Data", *Wall Street Journal*, 9 August 2010].

Q. And what about Edward Snowden's leaks?

A. Andrew Parker, director-general of Britain's MI5, commented in 2013: "It causes enormous damage to make public the reach and limits of GCHQ techniques. Such information hands the advantage to the terrorists. It is the gift they need to evade us and strike at will." [quoted Tom Whitehead, *Daily Telegraph*, 9 October 2013]. In 2014 former US Secretary of State Hillary Clinton commented: "I have a hard time thinking that somebody who is a champion of privacy and liberty has taken refuge in Russia, under Putin's authority." ["Hillary Clinton: Edward Snowden's Leaks Helped Terrorists", NationalJournal.com, 25 April 2014].

Right to Life

Q. Does your right to life mean that the state will step in to protect you if your life is seriously in danger?
A. You should be so lucky! In a 2012 case the UK Supreme Court held that an NHS Trust should have protected a woman from the "real and immediate" risk of suicide even though she was a voluntary patient. [*Rabone v. Pennine Care NHS Trust* [2012] UKSC 2]. The "real and immediate" risk of suicide is now the test for this kind of case – as against the previous test of "gross negligence". Both these tests are lamentably vague, which tends to be the case with judge-made criteria.
Q. Do the police still have immunity from negligence claims if they fail to arrest someone after receiving warnings about them?
A. In *Osman v. UK* [1998] 29 EHRR 245, involving a killing and a serious wounding after a long series of bizarre incidents, the Strasbourg court held that the police immunity established by the House of Lords case *Hill v. Chief Constable of West Yorkshire* [1989] AC 53 was contrary to ECHR Article

6 (fair trial), although not to Article 2 (right to life). However, the law has not been changed and the police immunity therefore still stands, although it has been called into question in certain extreme situations by the High Court in *DSD v. Commissioner of the Police for the Metropolis* [2014] EWHC 436 (QB).

Q. Police immunity from suit is quite an important matter. Why is there no legislation about it?

A. Good point. I'll come back later to Parliament's dereliction of duty by failing to clarify and regulate the law by legislation.

Q. What about self-defence?

A. That's another area where the law is unclear.

Q. But there the law has actually been changed, hasn't it?

A. The outcry over the way Tony Martin was treated, being initially charged with murder for killing an intruder, eventually led to an amendment of the law by Parliament. Section 43 of the Crime and Courts Act 2013 now allows you as a householder to use "disproportionate force" against an intruder provided you believe that the amount of force that you have used is "reasonable" in the circumstances, as long as the amount of force is not "grossly disproportionate". This leaves it up to the courts to decide what was in the mind of the householder and then to distinguish between "disproportionate" and "grossly disproportionate" force, arguably a distinction without a difference. And leaving this kind of decision to the courts is bound to lead to uncertainty and repeated appeals. Parliament should legislate, but it should legislate clearly and decisively.

Torture

Q. But what's wrong with the courts interpreting the law? That's what judges are supposed to do, isn't it?

A. The trouble is that "interpretation" can easily morph into legislation, which is a no-no for judges.

Q. Can you give me an example?

A. Cases brought by terror suspects objecting to deportation are good examples.

Q. In what way?

A. Terror suspects regularly claim that they are in danger of being tortured if sent back to their country of origin. So the courts generally stop the UK from deporting them without ironclad assurances from the countries concerned.

Q. It's nice to be kind, isn't it?

A. Kind to whom? Allowing potentially dangerous people to remain in Britain on the loose puts the British population at risk. The rights of the law-abiding majority must never be lost sight of. And why should Britain be responsible for what a foreign country does?

Q. But isn't the UK obliged under ECHR Article 3 to prevent torture?

A. What ECHR 3 says is: "No one shall be subjected to torture or to inhuman or degrading treatment or punishment." It's addressed to the signatory states, including the UK. So, what it means is simply that the UK must not subject anyone to torture, etc. Moreover, ECHR Article 1 stipulates that "The High Contracting Parties [i.e. the signatory states including the UK] shall secure to everyone within their jurisdiction the rights and freedoms defined in Section 1 of this Convention" – i.e. the substantive rights, including those in Article 3. This makes it clear that the UK's obligations under the ECHR are limited to its own territory. It is wrong under international law for a state to impose obligations on other states. "The first and foremost restriction imposed by international law on a State is that…it may not exercise its power in any form in the territory of another State." [Permanent Court of International Justice (predecessor of the International Court of Justice), 1923].

Q But isn't the reason the UK courts have adopted the "politically correct" approach to deportation -- *non-refoulement*, as it is called -- simply their obligation to follow the decisions of the European Court of Human Rights in Strasbourg?

A. No, that's wrong for two reasons. First, the domestic UK courts are not bound to follow Strasbourg slavishly. In the words of former Lord Chancellor Lord (Derry) Irvine, the architect of the Human Rights Act, the UK domestic have proceeded "on the false premise that they are bound (or as good as bound) to follow any clear decision of the European Court of Human Rights which is relevant to a case before them." [Lord Irvine, "A British Interpretation of Convention Rights", lecture 14 December 2011]. But in fact, as section 2(1)(a) of the Human Rights Act makes plain, the domestic courts' duty is only to "take into account" judgments, decisions etc. of the Strasbourg court.

Q. And what's the second reason?

A. The second reason is that, in regard to *non-refoulement* cases, the Strasbourg court has now softened its position while the UK courts have still stuck to the old hard-line approach. Here's what the Strasbourg court said in *Babar Ahmad & Abu Hamza (Othman) v UK* [2012] ECHR 609: "The absolute nature of Article 3 does not mean that any form of ill treatment will act as a bar to removal from a Contracting State......This court has repeatedly stated that the Convention does not purport to be a means of requiring the contracting states to impose convention standards on other states....This being so, treatment which might violate Article 3 because of an act or omission of a contracting state might not attain the minimum level of severity which is required for there to be a violation of Article 3 in an expulsion or extradition case."[§177]. Yet the UK courts continue to apply a "politically correct" approach, as in the 2016 SIAC decision refusing to allow six Algerians to be deported for "lack of a robust system of verification" of assurances received from Algeria: *BB v. Secretary of State for the Home Department SC/39/2005* [See Chapter 4].

Q. I note that the Government lamely accepted this decision. Instead of appealing to another court, is there anything the Government can do to stop the courts from blocking its anti-terror security policy?

A. In fact, there is. On the basis of parliamentary sovereignty, the Government can put through Parliament legislation to reverse a court decision. The best-known example of this is the War Damage Act 1965, an Act of Parliament with retroactive force passed to overturn the decision of the House of Lords (then the highest court) in *Burmah Oil v. Lord Advocate* [1965] AC 75.

Judge-made law

Q. The rule of law is one of the most important principles of the British constitution, isn't it?

A. Yes, but only in theory. It doesn't really exist in practice.

Q. But it's constantly proclaimed by the government, judges, lawyers, academics, and civil liberties organizations alike.

A. "A government not of men but of laws." Is that what you're talking about?

Q. Precisely. Isn't that what we have?

A. Unfortunately not. Laws are only words on paper. How can they rule?

Q. So what really exists?

A. A government not of laws but of lawyers – or, to be precise, of judges.

Q. Please explain.

A. As laws are just words on paper, they need to be interpreted. That's where the judges come in.

Q. Lord Denning was frequently rapped over the knuckles for overstepping the mark, I know.

His "purposive interpretation" of statute law was reversed by the House of Lords on the ground that it was "a naked usurpation of the legislative function under the thin disguise of interpretation". But that was over half a century ago. Things have moved on since then, haven't they?

A. The Sovereignty of Parliament is still the bedrock principle of the British Constitution. This principle was reaffirmed by both the High Court and the UK Supreme Court in the "Brexit" case of 2016-17. It is a usurpation of the power of Parliament for judges to make law, because that is legislation.

Q. So why has Parliament failed to pass legislation to protect privacy and to clarify the law in so many other difficult areas, like negligence for example?

A. Unfortunately, the UK Government and Parliament have for a very long time been guilty of a dereliction of duty. Parliamentary sovereignty gives Parliament (and therefore in practice the Government) great power, but it also gives them an obligation to clarify and regulate the law by legislation.

Q. Doesn't Parliament's failure to legislate leave a vacuum?

A. It certainly does, so it's not surprising that the judges have stepped into that vacuum and made law themselves, which they are not meant to do.

Q. So, why is there a feeling that Parliament makes too much law? For example, on 18 January 2017 the House of Lords, the upper house of Parliament, had a debate on "parliamentary proceedings" introduced by Lord Butler of Brockwell, a former Cabinet Secretary (head of the UK Home Civil Service), who said: "There is a widespread feeling that, under pressure from the Executive, Parliament makes too much law. To give one illustration, in 2010 legislation covering 2,700 pages was added to the statute book."

A. I'm afraid this rather gets hold of the wrong end of the stick. There *is* a proliferation of statutes, but that's because every little thing gets its own Act of Parliament. So, for example, if Parliament decided to criminalize spitting in public, that would be done by a separate statute called the Spitting in Public Act, which would contain a good few sections defining the meaning of "in public" and numerous Schedules listing which previous laws were being amended by this new statute.

Q. So what's the solution?

A. The solution is to codify the law.

Q. But there is already a certain amount of codification, isn't there?

A. Yes, but only a very limited amount, like company law, for example.

Q. I thought there was a plan to codify English law?

A. Supposedly. There was a petition to the Prince Regent as long ago as 1818 for codification of statute law. In 1992 the English Law Commission had a firm recommendation: "Codification of English criminal law is urgently needed" [Consultation Paper No. 127]. In 1989 they had even produced a draft Criminal Code Bill. And what happened? Nothing. In the Law Commission's 2009 "Newsletter" it was reported that the Law Commission was again working on a Criminal Law Code.

Q. Would you include codification of the common law?

A. Absolutely.

Q. But wouldn't that destroy the flexibility of the common law?

A. What it would destroy, or at least help to destroy, is the serious muddle in which the common law is now plunged.

Q. In what respect?

A. In numerous respects. When judges make law, which is what is happening more and more, it is bound to be unclear and there are bound to be serious disagreements between the judges on what the law is.

Q. Can you give me an example?

A. The current test for a duty of care in the tort of negligence, for example, is (a) reasonable foreseeability, (b) proximity, and (c) it must be "fair, just and reasonable" to impose liability. This is just hopelessly vague, leaving it to individual judges to decide. Or take prenuptial agreements, which are recognized by statute in most US states and in many other countries. But in the UK it is up to a judge to decide whether to recognize a prenuptial agreement or not.

Q. But what is wrong with giving judges wide discretion in decision-making? They are professionals who decide cases without bias, aren't they?

A. With the best will in the world, it's impossible for anyone, including judges, to divest themselves entirely of their unconscious biases. Lord Neuberger, the president of the UK Supreme Court, made a rare admission in a 2015 speech to the Criminal Justice Alliance. Referring to judges, he said: "I dare say that we all suffer from a degree of unconscious bias, and it can occur in all sorts of manifestations.

It is almost by definition an unknown unknown, and therefore extraordinarily difficult to get rid of, or even to allow for." [www.supremecourt.uk–10 April 2015]. Strangely enough, however, the bias that Lord Neuberger appears to have been thinking of is against the poor, the uneducated and foreigners, whereas the bias that is actually manifested by some -- but not all -- judges is a "liberal" or even "politically correct" bias that has become dominant in the "chattering class", favouring groups perceived to be disadvantaged or subject to prejudice, including women, minorities, the disabled, gays and "trans" people. In addition, there is a much more puzzling tendency among judges -- with some notable exceptions -- to favour terror suspects, asylum seekers and even convicted killers.

Q. Is this why you think it's inadvisable to allow judges too much power?

A. Precisely. This impacts directly not only on Government anti-terrorism policy but also on *your* rights as a law-abiding member of society.

"Political Correctness"

Q. How does "political correctness" (PC) impact my human rights?

A. It has a pretty severe impact on freedom of expression, for one thing. The "Support Gay Marriage" cake discussed earlier on is a good example, where a Christian bakery's refusal to make a cake with that slogan on it was held to amount to unlawful anti-gay discrimination.

Q. Which violated the bakers' right to freedom of religion under ECHR Article 9 and also their right as a business to refuse a specific order. But I don't quite see how it impacted their right to freedom of expression.

A. It essentially forced the bakers to promote gay marriage and did not let them express their opposition to it. It remains to be seen how this case fares in the UK Supreme Court and also possibly in Strasbourg.

Q. This effectively gives gays not just equality but special privileges, doesn't it?

A. Absolutely. That's why I say that the Equality Act 2010 should really be called the Special Privileges Act. See Chapter 7.

Suggested Solution

Q. So, what is your suggested solution to the muddled state of UK human rights law?

A. The first thing to understand is that, contrary to all the pro-Brexit propaganda, Britain's leaving the EU is not going to improve matters in the slightest.

Q. How so?

A. The ECHR politically correct "mission creep" did originate to quite a large extent with the Strasbourg court, but it was enthusiastically adopted by the UK domestic judges although they were not obliged to do more than "take into account" Strasbourg jurisprudence. And it is now clear that Brexit will not entail Britain's withdrawal from the ECHR or from the jurisdiction of the Strasbourg court. [Brexit will result in the UK not being subject to the jurisdiction of that other, more powerful court, the European Court of Justice (Court of Justice of the European Union), but that is not really relevant, although that court is becoming increasingly involved in human rights cases].

Q. What about the Human Rights Act (HRA)?

A. There's a lot of confusion about that. The HRA, which enshrines most of the articles of the ECHR, is essentially the vehicle for incorporating the ECHR into UK law, enabling the ECHR to be applied directly by any UK court or tribunal without the necessity for the case to go to Strasbourg, although a case can still be taken to Strasbourg after all domestic remedies have been exhausted.

Q. What will happen if the HRA is replaced by a British Bill of Rights, as the Conservative Party has been proposing for years?

A. The ECHR will still be relevant, but it will not then be part of UK law, and it will not be possible to apply to the Strasbourg court until all domestic remedies have been exhausted.

Q. So, will the ECHR still have a role alongside the British Bill of Rights?

A. Presumably, unless the UK withdraws from the ECHR. But, if it doesn't there is likely to be a clash between the ECHR and the British Bill of Rights. Needless to say, this has not been thought out by the Government!

Q. All those hypothetical matters aside, what practical steps do you recommend to reduce the muddle in which human rights law is now mired?

A. The first and most important thing is to repeal the part of the Constitutional Reform Act 2005 that subordinates the Executive to the judiciary.

Q. What provision is that?

A. Section 17 of the 2005 Act actually contains an oath that has to be taken by the Lord Chancellor (on behalf of the Government) to "respect the rule of law [and] defend the independence of the judiciary".

Q. What's wrong with that? After all, the judiciary and the executive are coequal branches of the government, aren't they?

A. Yes, supposedly. But notice that the government must defend the independence of the judiciary without any reciprocal duty on the part of the judiciary. And by "independence" is really meant "unelected and responsible to nobody".

Q. So, do you think judges should be elected?

A. Well, the majority of state judges in the US are elected, which I think is excellent. That would never be possible in the UK, but some sort of democratic confirmation -- possibly by Parliament, similar to confirmation of US Supreme Court judges by the Senate -- would be a big improvement on the very opaque system now in force.

Q. I thought UK judges were appointed by the government?

A. That used to be the arrangement, which was fairer because of the doctrine of the separation of powers with checks and balances, which is supposed to be a basic UK constitutional principle.

Q. Supposed to be?
A. Yes, I'm afraid judicial power has grown so much that there is disagreement even about the basics. Here, for example, is an incorrect constitutional formulation stated as definitive by Lord Justice Nolan: "The proper constitutional relationship of the executive with the courts is that the courts will respect all acts of the executive within its lawful province, and that the executive will respect all decisions of the courts as to what its lawful province is." [*M. v. Home Office* [1992] QB 270 at 314].
Q. What's wrong with that formulation?
A. It wrongly subordinates the executive completely to the judges. The courts are here erroneously given the power to determine the contents and extent of executive power – which is legislation and therefore belongs to Parliament, not to the courts. And the executive is given the slavish role of having to accept whatever crumbs the judges decide to allow them.
Q. What would be a more accurate formulation?
A. Lord Mustill's formulation in *R v. Home Secretary ex parte Fire Brigades Union* [1995] 2 AC 513 at 567: "Parliament has a legally unchallengeable right to make whatever laws it thinks right. The executive carries on the administration of the country in accordance with the powers conferred on it by law. The courts interpret the laws and see that they are obeyed."

****

Index

"Act of State" doctrine, 107
A et al, Mahmoud Abu Rideh, Jamal Ajouaou v. Secretary of State for the Home Department [2004], 236
A v UK [1998], 91
A(FC) v. Secretary of State for the Home Department [2004], 45
Abortion, 78, 79, 80, 81
Abortion Act 1967, 78, 79
Abu Hamza, 34, 97, 104, 262
Abu Qatada, 34, 57
Academic Freedom, 124, 126
AF v. Secretary of State for the Home Department [2009], 52
Afghanistan, 72, 73
Age, 25, 126
Al-Sweady Inquiry, 89
American Declaration of Independence, 10
Amnesty International, 205, 206, 257
Ann Widdecombe, 29, 166, 167, 186
Aristotle, 9
Armed Forces Act 2006, 73
Assisted Suicide, 76
Associated Provincial Picture Houses v. Wednesbury [1948], 230

Babar Ahmad & Abu Hamza (Othman) v UK [2012, 104
Babar Ahmad and Abu Hamza Othman v. UK [2012], 97

Baroness Deech, 166, 167, 168, 189, 190, 195
Belhaj v. Straw [2017], 41, 105
Belief, 25
Bloody Friday, 71
Bloody Sunday, 69, 71
Boy Scouts of America, 138
Brandenburg v. Ohio (1968), 116
Brexit, 4, 14, 34, 40, 60, 98, 105, 201, 264, 268
Brind v. Secretary of State for the Home Department [1991], 229
British Constitution, 38, 264
British Scout Association, 138
Brown v. Board of Education (1954), 171
Bull v. Hall [2013], 28
Burmah Oil v. Lord Advocate [1965], 105, 263
Burton v. Islington Health Authority (1992), 82

Calcutt committee, 145
CCTV cameras, 165
Cecil John Rhodes, 126
Chahal v. UK [1996], 48, 94
Charlie Hebdo, 128, 129
Charter of Fundamental Rights of the European Union, 60, 159
Christine Goodwin v. UK [2002], 139
Cicero, 8, 9

Clunis v. Camden & Islington Health Authority (1998), 61
Coco v. A.N. Clark (Engineers) Ltd [1969], 148
Common Law Rights, 17, 234
Constitutional Reform Act 2005, 39
Corporal Punishment, 90, 91
Court of Appeal, 20, 27, 39, 63, 64, 76, 81, 107, 117, 133, 147, 148, 158, 159, 161, 190, 191, 208, 224, 226, 227, 235, 237, 239, 242, 254
Crime and Courts Act 2013, 64, 259
Criminal Justice Alliance, 36, 174, 210, 266
Crown in Parliament, 14
Curia Regis, 22

Data Retention and Investigatory Powers Act (DRIPA) 2014, 158
David Cameron, 70, 129, 130, 155, 172, 187
Defamation Act 2013, 112, 224
Delfi v. Estonia [(2015), 113
Denmark, France, Norway, Sweden & the Netherlands v Greece, 88
Derry Irvine, 51
Director of Public Prosecutions (DPP), 77
Disability, 25, 26
Disability Discrimination Act 1995, 26
Donald Trump, 4

Donoghue v. Stevenson [1932], 11, 241
Douglas v. Hello! (2001), 147
Dunbar v. Plant [1997], 76
Duport Steels v. Sirs [1980], 38

Eckersley v. Mersey Docks [1891-94], 207
Edelman Trust Barometer, 157
Edward I, 25
Emmeline Pankhurst, 85
Emperor Justinian's, 16
Employment, 119, 168, 230, 231, 232, 234
Employment Appeal Tribunal, 119, 231, 232
Employment Tribunal, 119, 231, 232, 234
Equality Act 2010, 25, 27, 44, 223, 230, 231, 232, 268
Espionage Act of 1917, 115
European Convention on Human Rights, 4, 30, 33, 73
European Court of Human Rights, 4, 30, 42, 51, 66, 134, 152, 212, 261
Extradition Act 1870, 93

Fathers' Rights, 80
Feminism, 174
Fidel Castro, 123
Freedom of Expression, 3, 109, 143, 222, 223
French Revolution, 170

Gay Marriage, 27, 133, 225, 267
Gender dysphoria, 140

Gender reassignment, 25
Gender Recognition Act 2004, 139
General Augusto Pinochet, 205
Geneva Convention, 73
Glass Ceiling, 181
Gorden Kaye v Robertson [1990], 20
Gordon Brown, 25
Government Equalities Office, 186
Greek Case [(1969), 88

Habeas corpus, 19
Habeas Corpus Act 1679, 19
Halford v. United Kingdom ([1997], 146
Hammond v. Department of Public Prosecutions [2004], 118
Hate Speech, 119
Hatton v. UK (2003), 240
Heczegfalvy v Austria (1993), 90
Hillary Rodham Clinton., 122
Holman v. Johnson (1775), 62
House of Commons Women and Equalities Committee, 136, 187
Howell v. Lees-Millais [2007], 208
Human Fertilisation and Embryology Act 1990, 79
Human Rights Act 1998, 30, 119, 146

Ian Huntley, 218
Independent Press Standards Organisation (Ipso), 146

Infant Life (Preservation) Act 1929, 79, 81
Investigatory Powers Act 2016, 154, 158
Iraq Historic Allegations Team (IHAT), 73
Islamic State, 46
Isle of Man, 90

Jackson reforms, 201, 202
James Bulger, 55, 211, 217, 218
Jeremy Bentham, 10
John Adams, 49, 198
Jon Venables, 211

Kaye v. Robertson [1991], 144, 254
Keenan v. UK [2001], 62
Kelly v. Kelly (1997), 81
Kelly v. UK (1993), 68
Kerensky Syndrome, 45
King John, 22
Ku Klux Klan, 116

Larry Summers, 124, 126, 168, 178
Lee v. McArthur [2016], 27, 133
Libel, 110
Liberace v. Daily Mirror (1959), 111
Liberty, 10, 50, 51, 53, 54, 55, 56, 57, 58
London Borough of Lewisham v. Malcolm [2008], 26
Lord Kitchener, 84, 175
Lord Saville, 69, 70
Lord Woolf, 70, 214

M v. Home Office [1992], 39
M. v. Home Office [1992, 271
Magna Carta, 21, 22, 23, 25, 34, 57
Magor & St Mellons Rural DC v. Newport Corp [1952, 14
Marine Le Pen, 122
Massachusetts Constitution, 50, 198
Matrimonial Proceedings & Property Act 1970, 189
Max Mosley v. News Group Newspapers [2008], 112
Maxine Carr, 218, 219
McCann v. UK (1996), 66
McDonalds v. Steel and Morris [1997], 111
McKay v. Essex Area Health Authority (1982), 82
McLibel case, 111
Mental Health Act 1983, 63
Metropolitan International Schools v. Google [2009], 113
Migration Watch UK, 164
Military Service Act 1916, 84
Ministry of Defence, 68, 69, 226
Montreal Tramways Co. v. Leveillé (1933), 83
Mosley v. News Group Newspapers [2008], 150
Ms B v. An NHS Hospital Trust (2002), 77
MTE-Index v. Hungary [2016], 113

National Crime Agency (NCA), 155
National Security, 21

Natural Justice, 198, 205
Natural rights, 8, 10

OBG v. Allan [2007], 148, 150, 240
Offences Against the Person Act 1861, 82
Operation Northmoor, 73
Osborn v. Parole Board [2013], 17
Osman v. United Kingdom [(1998), 61

Parliamentary Defence Sub-Committee, 74
Planned Parenthood v. Casey (1992), 188
Planned Parenthood v. Danforth (1976), 188
Plessy v. Ferguson (1896), 171
Police Service of Northern Ireland (PSNI), 74
Porter v. Magill [2002], 207
Prenuptial agreements, 20, 169, 196
Prenuptial Contract, 20
President Trump, 130, 257
Press Complaints Commission, 145, 255
Presumption of innocence, 19
Pretty v. UK [2002], 76
Public Interest Lawyers (PIL), 74
Public Nudity, 118
Public Order Act 1986, 116, 117, 118, 123, 223, 225

Quotas, 29

R (Evans) v. Attorney General [2015], 14, 200
R (Fire Brigades Union) v. Secretary of State for the Home Department [1995], 39
R (Justice for Health Ltd) v. Secretary of State for Health [2016], 248
R (Miller) v. Secretary of State for Exiting the European Union [2016], 15
R (on the application of Bulger) v Secretary of State [2001], 218
R (Osborn) v. Parole Board [2013], 239
R (Pinochet Ugarte) v. Bow Street Metropolitan Stipendiary Magistrate (No. 2) [1999], 206
R (Smith) v. Secretary of State for Defence [1995], 226
R (Ullah) v. Special Adjudicator [2004], 37
R v. Anthony Edward Martin [2001], 64
R v. Home Secretary ex parte Fire Brigades Union [1995], 271
R v. Sussex Justices, ex parte McCarthy [1924], 216
R. v. Tait (1989), 81
Rabone v. Pennine Care NHS Trust [2012], 63, 258
Race, 25, 119, 172
Racial Discrimination, 171
Radmacher v. Granatino [2010], 193

Railway Ltd v. ASLEF [2016], 243
Recusal Rules, 207
Religion, 25
Reynolds v. Times Newspapers [1999], 223
Rhodes Scholarships, 126
Right To A Fair Trial, 198
Right to remain silent, 7
Right to Strike, 241
Right to vote in elections, 7
Rights of the Unborn Child, 81
Robert Thompson, 211
Roe v. Wade (1973), 79
Rule of Fairness, 221
Rule of Law, 49, 198

Saadi v. Italy (2008), 95
Sadam Hussain, 102
Savage v. South Essex Partnership [2008], 63
Secretary of State for Home Dept v. David Davis & Tom Watson, 158
Self-Defence, 63
Separation of Powers, 38
Sex, 25, 28, 29, 142, 167, 170, 185
Sex Discrimination (Election Candidates) Act 2002, 186
Sex Discrimination (Election Candidates) Act 2002,, 28
Sex Discrimination Act 1975, 28, 29, 167, 185
Sexual orientation, 26
Sir Michael Fallon, 73
Sir Oswald Mosley, 112, 151
Sir William Blackstone, 16
Slander, 110

Slavery, 8
Smith & Grady v. UK (1999), 227
Soering v. UK (1989), 48
Soering v. UK [(1989), 93
Solicitors Disciplinary Tribunal, 74
Sovereignty of Parliament, 14, 15, 33, 38, 104, 241, 264
Speaker's Corner, 109
Special Air Service (SAS), 66
Special Immigration Appeal Commission, 47
Special Immigration Appeals Commission (SIAC), 97, 235
St Thomas Aquinas, 9
Stanford Encyclopedia of Philosophy, 7
Strike Ballots, 246
Suffragettes, 167, 186
Suicide Act 1961, 77
Super-injunctions, 112
Supreme Court of Canada, 83
Synthetic babies, 130

Taliban, 72

Theresa May, 34, 35, 41, 74, 98, 108, 130, 131, 172, 173, 187
Tolley v. Fry [1931], 111
Torture 87
Trade Union and Labour Relations (Consolidation) Act 1992, 246
Transgender, 136, 137, 140
Trial by Jury, 23

Unconscious Bias, 36, 210
United Nations Convention against Torture (CAT, 236
US Bureau of Labor Statistics, 183

Venables & Thompson v. News Group Newspapers [2001], 215
Villar v. Gilbey (1907), 83

War Damage Act 1965, 40, 105, 262
Wednesbury unreasonable, 226, 229
Widgery report, 69